D0742052

DATE DUE

JUN 8 '91			
GAYLORD			PRINTED IN U.S.A.

Marcus Foster and the
Oakland Public Schools

This volume is sponsored by the
OAKLAND PROJECT
University of California, Berkeley

Marcus Foster and the
Oakland Public Schools

Leadership in an Urban Bureaucracy

Jesse J. McCorry

UNIVERSITY OF CALIFORNIA PRESS
BERKELEY   LOS ANGELES   LONDON

University of California Press
Berkeley and Los Angeles, California

University of California Press, Ltd.
London, England

ISBN 0-520-03397-3
Library of Congress Catalog Card Number: 76-55567
Printed in the United States of America

1 2 3 4 5 6 7 8 9 0

The Oakland Project

At a time when much is said but little is done about the university's relationship to urban problems, it is useful for those who are looking for ways of relating the university to the city to take a brief look at the Oakland Project of the University of California, which combined policy analysis, service to city officials and community groups, action in implementing proposals, training of graduate students, teaching new undergraduate courses, and scholarly studies of urban politics. The "university" is an abstraction, and as such it exists only for direct educational functions, not for the purpose of doing work within cities. Yet there are faculty members and students who are willing to devote large portions of their time and energy to investigating urban problems and to making small contributions toward resolving them. Our cities, however, do not need an invasion of unskilled students and professors. There is no point in hurtling into the urban crisis unless one has some special talent to contribute. After all, there are many people in city government—and even more on street corners—who are less inept than untrained academics. University people must offer the cities the talent and resources which they need and which they could not get otherwise.

In 1965 a group of graduate students and faculty members at the University of California at Berkeley became involved in a program of policy research and action in the neighboring city of

Oakland. As members of the Oakland Project, they tried to meet some of the city's most pressing analytical needs and also to make suggestions that could be implemented.

Members of the project made substantial time commitments (usually about two years) to working in a particular Oakland city agency. Normal working time was two days a week, although special crisis situations in the city sometimes necessitated much larger blocks of time. Since project members worked with city officials and remained in the city to help implement the suggestions they made, they avoided the "hit-and-run" stigma that members of city agencies often attach to outsiders. By attempting first to deal with problems as city officials understand them, project members developed the necessary confidence to be asked to undertake studies with broader implications.

The Oakland Project became a point of communication for individuals and groups in the city of Oakland and throughout the University of California. Its focus expanded from a concentration on city budgeting to a wide range of substantive policies and questions of political process; for example, revenue, police, personnel, federal aid, education, libraries, and the institutionalization of policy analysis. The Project provided assistance to governmental (mayor, city manager, chief of police, head of civil service, superintendent of schools) and nongovernmental (community group) actors. In order to transmit the knowledge gained, Oakland Project members taught courses—open to both undergraduate and graduate students—dealing with urban problems and policies. The Project's scholarly objective is to improve policy analysis by providing new ways of understanding decisions and outcomes that affect cities. Its members have based numerous research essays on their experience in the city. It is hoped that the books in this series will be another means of transmitting what they have learned to a wider audience.

Contents

Preface

This study is a product of my participation in the Oakland Project at the University of California, Berkeley. When I joined the Project in the summer of 1969, I never expected that my acquaintance with Marcus Foster, then an associate superintendent in the Philadelphia schools, would become such an important part of my work.

I met Marcus Foster in Washington, D.C., in 1968, two years before he was to become the superintendent of schools in Oakland, California. At the time I was working for Project Upward Bound, one of the anti-poverty programs of the Office of Economic Opportunity (OEO). A primary objective of Upward Bound was to demonstrate that so-called disadvantaged students in secondary schools could succeed in higher education provided certain systematic institutional and instructional changes were made. Toward this end, OEO wanted to create an advisory council consisting of principals whose schools were active in Upward Bound. An advisory council, we believed, would make it easier to persuade high schools to be more cooperative in this effort. We also anticipated that such a body could help to strengthen our position in seeking more funds from Congress or in bargaining with OEO.

Foster, a high school principal in Philadelphia at the time, shared our belief in the potential value of an advisory council and was happy to become a member. However, we never learned what his participation might have produced, for shortly after our initial Washington meeting he became an associate superintendent of schools in Philadelphia. Consequently, he was ineligible to continue as a council member. But Foster's acceptance of our invitation and his strong support for constituency organization (such as the advisory council) reflected his belief in the ability of an organized clientele group to stimulate organizational change. What we were proposing for an advisory council was but an extension of the kinds of things which Marcus Foster had done as a high school principal.

Our interest in Foster, however, had little to do with his political knowledge and skill. Indeed, I don't remember that any of us ever raised such questions. Rather, we were impressed by his willingness to try something new in an effort to improve the academic performance of non-white and poor central-city students. Moreover, we were interested in the deliberate steps he had taken to open up his school to the larger community as he sought the resources to make necessary improvements.

Though a member of a large bureaucracy, Foster nonetheless maintained a somewhat anti-bureaucratic stance. He believed that public organizations could be changed if talented and committed people from the inside joined with organizational publics and worked cooperatively toward agreed-upon goals.

After our one-day meeting in Washington in 1968, I did not see Marcus Foster again until he arrived in Oakland in 1970. However, because my job required me to keep abreast of educational issues, I was able to keep in contact with Foster's career. There were, after all, only a handful of blacks occupying significant positions in public education, and the informal communications network between blacks inside and outside the OEO programs were frequently used. I left Washington in the summer of 1969 to begin graduate work in political science at Berkeley. By the midsummer of 1969 the Oakland school system was the center of a growing political controversy. School board members had known since the previous year that a new superintendent would have to be found to replace their outgoing political executive. Although the board had tried earlier to fill the post of superintendent, it had been unsuccessful. But, it was the very lack of success which turned the issue of executive succession into a stormy conflict over community involvement. And, like such controversies in other big cities where blacks perceived a political opportunity, there was strong pressure on the Board of Education to select a black person for the position. Moreover the board members showed some inclination to do so. A graduate student working for one member of the board asked me specifically if I knew of any black educators who might be interested in the Oakland vacancy. I suggested Marcus Foster. At the time I did not know that at least one board member also knew of Foster. It was still a very pleasant surprise when "Marc" was selected some ten months later.

My own interests in urban education began to undergo some changes as a result of my graduate studies. Increasingly questions of organizational adaptability at the urban level presented themselves, as the Oakland school system sought to find a new superintendent in the midst of a growing community conflict. But adaptability is of interest not solely because of environmental pressures on a public organization. As I learned from my three years of watching Marcus Foster, pressure or stress may just as often be internally derived. To be sure, such sources are less likely to be publicly visible. However, the organization must adapt to stress, whether external or internal, and it must do so while its purposes continue to be served.

My opportunity to look more closely at the issue of adaptability came about when the Urban Institute asked several members of the Oakland Project to assist in a study of educational finance. The study was just getting underway when Marcus Foster assumed office. From my point of view, this appointment was a stroke of good luck! When I approached Marc with a request to use the Oakland public schools in the study, his answer was a quick yes.

As it happened, the study was of limited value to the new superintendent. It did provide him with some information to strengthen his rebuttal to those critics who claimed that the schools discriminated against blacks in the allocation of resources. However, from Foster's point of view, the study did not help *him* to implement innovations. He wanted to find ways to help his organization adapt to his planned changes, and he had already made plans to change the budgetary practices which our study investigated.

Nevertheless, he allowed me to become virtually a member of

his cabinet, the principal decision-making group in his administration. At the same time, I was conducting the interviews for the finance study with various members of the school staff. Because I had some experience in dealing with community groups on educational questions, Foster sometimes used me as an assistant. These circumstances gave me an unusual degree of access to the workings of the Oakland public schools during Marc's tenure.

Oakland's new superintendent of schools did not hesitate to seize upon opportunities which he considered to be important to the achievement of his goals. He viewed the availability of graduate students in the Bay Area as just such an opportunity. Their assistance, especially if it were free, was regarded as a means of developing good relations with the several colleges and universities. He hoped that such relations would give him access to the expertise of the faculties at those institutions. It is a fair inference that Foster's generous reception of graduate students tacitly acknowledged some limitations on the part of the organization's staff and the superintendent knew that what he wanted to accomplish would not be easy.

But allowing me, as a participant-observer, to attend all the meetings of his cabinet (including the two "retreats") indicated a good bit about Marc's style. He was confident of his own ability to lead the school system, and his leadership was marked by a considerable openness. All of the cabinet members knew that I was taking notes and that some of the things said during those meetings would eventually become part of my dissertation. Yet no one raised an objection. Indeed, part of my function at the retreats was to keep a record for the summary on the final afternoon. And at the meeting at Marc's home when he named the members of his cabinet, my notes were his record of what was said and done. All of the quotations attributed to school staff members come from direct interviews or from the notes taken during cabinet meetings.

OPEN ADMINISTRATION OF ORGANIZATIONS

Foster's open leadership style was an explicit response to one of the most frequently heard criticisms of urban bureaucracies during the 1960s. However much the public might benefit from a political executive's candor and an open administration, they necessarily render the executive more vulnerable to criticism.

Marc expected, and got, his share of criticism. But he believed it was a small price to pay for the trust and confidence of the public, his staff and the Board of Education. And it was Foster's ability to inspire and maintain this support while attempting to institute the complex set of changes which became the hallmark of his administration.

The study which follows is an examination of Marcus Foster's leadership as he sought to guide the Oakland public schools through the adoption of several innovations. Each of these— community participation, decentralization, and a planning, programming and budgeting system—had been vigorously advocated by critics of traditional bureaucratic practices. However, not even the strongest advocates conceived of them in an integrated fashion. For the new superintendent there was no apparent reason why they should not form the basis for a comprehensive approach to organizational change. The problems of the urban schools were, in Foster's judgment, so closely interrelated that a particularistic approach would not begin to meet the challenge. Soon after Foster took over, his actions and statements suggested that the apparent intractability of the difficulties in urban school systems stemmed from too much reliance on narrowly focused attempts to institute change. For him, a comprehensive approach offered more potential for success. Foster wasted little time in getting started, as we shall see.

The following study is an examination of Marcus Foster's behavior as he tried to lead his organization to the adoption of the changes mentioned above. Foster's experiences with organizational change suggest that bureaucratic resistance may not be the villain which so many advocates of change claim it to be. Nor, it became clear to me, are a permissive environment and supportive constituency easily convertible into the kinds of resources which can facilitate organizational change.

Instead of seizing on the shibboleth of "bureaucratic recalcitrance" as the explanation of obstacles to change we should probe more deeply. One is likely to discover that the problem is a lack of knowledge. Despite their admitted expertise, organizations are not omniscient. There are things which they cannot accomplish. No amount of leadership can make up for organizational ignorance. This, for example, was the case with PPBS (planning, programming, budgeting system). Despite its attractiveness, no one knew how to turn the concept into a practical technique of management. Foster's belief in the innovation and his public support notwithstanding, PPBS exceeded the capacity of the organization. It is also important to recognize that organizations may fail to achieve some objectives because they lack sufficient control over the sources of the problem that change is supposed to address. Thus, improving the educational performance of students requires more than increasing the number of teachers. Organizational change in the schools will do little to affect a learning problem if the disability is tied to the distribution of wealth in society.

For organizational change to be successful it must be directed to those things an organization knows how to do, or can be taught to perform. This means that successful change will take place within the organization to the extent that it has control of the necessary resources and that the problem addressed is itself within the organization. Where the organization is not in control of the resources needed for successful change, to the extent that they exist, they must be brought in from the environment. In each case, there is an especial responsibility for leadership: the political executive sets the agenda for changing goals and objectives. Achieving these implies that the leader will know what is needed to accomplish what he or she wants the organization to do.

Marcus Foster was not entirely successful. But this should not be taken to mean that he was a failure. As I hope to make clear in the following pages, there are benefits to be had from "failed hopes."

This study would not have been possible without the generous support of Marcus Foster. I am sincerely grateful for the time and encouragement which he so freely gave. In addition, Robert Blackburn, the deputy superintendent of schools, shared many of his insights with me as he patiently answered innumerable questions. To the members of the superintendent's cabinet—Alden Badal, Edward Cockrum, the late Verdese Carter, Harry Reynolds, Leo Croce, Lee Panttaja and Rhoda Hollenbeck—I owe a particular debt of gratitude. There were also many other members of the schools' staff whom I cannot single out for thanks. I hope, however, that they know how much I appreciate their many kindnesses and assistance.

Several of my former teachers—Professors Aaron Wildavsky, Robert Biller, and Jack Citron—did all the things which are expected by graduate students, and more. They listened, gave advice, and guided in so many ways. To them goes much of the credit for whatever merit this study may possess. Inevitably, however, some of that advice was not taken; the errors which remain are my own.

Mary Ellen Anderson, who kept the Oakland Project administratively afloat, deserves a special note of thanks for seeing this study through several early drafts. Mrs. Lillian Ehrlich, at Washington University, did a heroic job of preparing the final manuscript.

My study of leadership and organization innovation ends on a tragic note. Marcus Foster was assassinated on November 6, 1973. To his memory this work is dedicated.

1

Introduction

On 6 April 1970 Marcus A. Foster became the twenty-fifth super-intendent of schools in Oakland, California, and the first black man to head a major urban school system. Acceptance of the Board of Education's four-year contract brought to a close almost eighteen months of board-community conflict. Despite the importance of that conflict, the process of its resolution is not the objective of this volume. Because the controversy surrounding political succession established the immediate environment of Foster's tenure, however, it is examined in chapter 2. It was Foster's skillful handling of school-community conflict and student unrest which made him an attractive prospect to Oakland's school board members. Indeed, the demonstration of these skills had figured in his rapid rise to a senior administrative position in Philadelphia.

Urban political violence had subsided by the time the new superintendent formally took office in July 1970. Nevertheless, the recent hostilities between elements of the school system's public and the organization was fresh in the public mind. Because Superintendent Foster was an unknown quantity and because he was a black "first," it is not surprising that his appointment evoked conflicting expectations. For many of the black activists, represented by the Oakland Black Caucus, Foster was a black pawn foisted on the community by a board which could not be trusted. The caucus also feared that a black political executive

1

was likely to be sabotaged by a predominantly white staff if he attempted to introduce changes implying a commitment to non-white interests. And, in terms of their own political self-interest, these articulate activists were wary of the new superintendent because he had refused to submit himself to their "screening."

For the board of education and many white constituents, on the other hand, the new superintendent represented the key to racial peace and the end of overt community conflicts. Foster was aware of these initial expectations but he also believed that there would be few problems in dealing with them.

But to Foster, the conflicting expectations were small matters. They would require his attention, to be sure. However, he believed there was an essential consensus among black and white parents that the Oakland schools were not effectively teaching their children. And the school head recognized that there were a number of Oakland citizens who were concerned about the rising costs of public education. The homeowners, many of whom no longer had children in the public schools, had consistently demonstrated that concern by refusing to approve tax increases. The first order of business for the new superintendent, then, was to gain the confidence and support of the diverse groups who were attentive to educational politics in Oakland.

Dr. Foster believed that a leadership style emphasizing personal accessibility, public visibility and rhetorical skill would show that a new administration was in charge of the Oakland public schools. This combination of characteristics was, in Foster's view, a way to make a symbolically effective response to demands for a more open administration. The superintendent wanted his style to be a sign of what the public could expect from the new administration. The issues of leadership style and executive constituency development are treated more fully in chapter 3.

The early style of leadership which Foster demonstrated in Oakland is reminiscent of the "agitator" described by Lasswell and Kaplan.[1] The superintendent unabashedly sought to evoke

---

1. In their effort to distinguish types of political leaders Harold D. Laswell and Abraham Kaplan observe: "The leader may be an *agitator* or *administrator*. He may place a high value on the sentimentalized response of the rank and file at large, or be more closely bound to particular individuals, concerned with coordinating the practices of the members of his immediate environment. He may rely upon the efficacy of symbols—formula and gesture, slogan and po-

an emotional response among the constituents of his organization. In doing so Foster believed that he would be able to transform these sentiments into support for his planned changes in the structure of the bureaucracy. Still, this potential generalized support would only provide a "permissive environment" for innovation. In order to create changes, in fact, Superintendent Foster would also have to demonstrate his ability in administration. Whether the two types of leadership, agitator and administrator, could be successfully combined was another of the problems which Foster would have to confront.

Organizational change does not take place in a vacuum. There are pressures, from within and from without, which require some adjustment of current structures and processes. Foster's attempt to deal, first, with the issue of community involvement reflected a concern about public organizations and their societal settings raised by V. O. Key, Jr., some years earlier:

. . . one of the great functions of the bureaucratic institutions is as a conservator of the values of a culture. In the purposes, procedures, ceremonies, outlook, and habits of the bureaucracy are formalized the traditional cultural values. Where the rub comes is when social purpose abruptly changes or becomes unclear or divided.[2]

For many urban bureaucracies during the sixties, participation and community involvement implied a redefinition of traditionally accepted values. Each, in the first instance, challenged the belief in the exclusive technical expertise of organizational members. But of perhaps greater importance was the growing demand for bureaucracies to become more representative of the diversity which made up their political environments. This latter demand threatened the long-standing attachment to the ideal of neutral competence in public organizations. Foster regarded these challenges as valid. For him, as for many of the activists, public

---

lemic—in transforming interpersonal relations, or place a corresponding emphasis on operations and organizational structures. And coordinate with these differences in identification and expectation may be differences in demand as well, the agitator orienting demands around remote and abstract goals, the administrator around the more immediate and concrete." *Power and Society: A Framework for Political Inquiry* (New Haven: Yale University Press, 1950), pp. 153-54.

2. V. O. Key, Jr., "Politics and Administration," in *The Future of Government in the United States: Essays in Honor of Charles E. Merriam*, ed. Leonard D. White (Chicago: University of Chicago Press, 1942), p. 160.

school systems deserved criticism for having performed too well as "conservators." The touted racial and cultural pluralism of American society was reflected in neither school curricula nor the composition of educational staffs. Black political mobilization in the area of educational politics focused on securing changes in these areas, as well as on the acquisition of decision-making roles in educational policy. Achievement of these goals was expected to make bureaucracies more sensitive to societal changes of purpose.

The goals sought through black political activism gave renewed emphasis to the need for a better understanding of the linkages between bureaucracies and the political systems which they help to sustain. Sensitivity to environmental changes, if it was to become a lasting characteristic of public organizations, would require an effective intelligence system, and more.[3] Bureaucracies would also have to reexamine the linkages, or as Ralph Braibanti put it, "ecological relationships," to their sociopolitical settings.[4] In part, it was the failure to understand the political relevance of these relationships which produced the black demands for community control. Foster believed that his own initial activities would indicate his awareness of the ecologi-

3. Obviously few urban bureaucracies can afford the sophisticated means available to the federal government or private organizations for obtaining information about their environments. However as we shall see, there may be alternative ways in which this critical organizational need can be met. The best general work on this subject remains Harold Wilensky, *Organizational Intelligence* (New York: Basic Books, 1967).

4. This relationship has more recently been of interest to scholars concerned with "development administration." For example, Ralph Braibanti extended the point made by Key when he stated: "There is no questions that the administrative system has an ecological relationship with the total social order, that it is influenced by it, and that often it cannot contribute to balanced political development unless its . . . capability is articulated to the political growth process in some manner. Moreover, . . . in the long run, an administrative apparatus must be sustained by doctrinal or ideological supports derived from the social order." Ralph Braibanti, "Administrative Reform in the Context of Political Growth," in *Frontiers of Development Administration*, ed. Fred W. Riggs (Durham: Duke University Press, 1971), p. 229.

In the field of urban politics this relationship has most often been subsumed under the rubric of "political ethos." Similarly one may find discussions of Key's conservator function within the context of analyses of political culture. For an illustration see Raymond E. Wolfinger and John Osgood Field, "Political Ethos and the Structure of City Government," *American Political Science Review* 60, no. 2 (June 1966): 306-26; Edward Banfield and James Q. Wilson also allude to this relation in their *City Politics* (New York: Random House, 1963).

cal relation. The superintendent expected that the changes he would introduce—community involvement, a decentralized decision-making structure, and the planning, programming and budgeting system—would be firm evidence of that awareness.

Dr. Foster's task was not simply organizational change. His efforts were akin to the purposes ascribed by Martin Landau to institution-building in poor countries where

> an organization will be able to operate effectively in its immediate task environment to the extent that its distinguishing properties are distributed throughout the system of which it is a member. This distribution must be a prime objective for any institution-building program and it is quite literally, an educational objective. For when such properties . . . are widely distributed, there exists the basis for a matching, a pairing of codes [sender and receiver each understand the message symbols, forms and content] which renders the relationship between an organization and its environment less uncertain . . . ends and means are correlated.[5]

Thus, Oakland's new educational leader sought to educate his public and his staff in the "distinguishing properties" of the institution he planned to develop. While his first change, community participation or sharing power with constituents, might mitigate charges of bureaucratic isolation and inaccessibility, Superintendent Foster did not view this single innovation as the solution to the problems of urban education.[6] He recognized that public estrangement from bureaucracy was only one source of environmental hostility and discontent. For some among the school system's public the problem was one of long standing: economy and efficiency in government. Among this group we find the various economic interests in Oakland who were concerned about the general economic growth of the city. In their judgment a good school system helps to promote such growth, a

5. Martin Landau, "Linkage, Coding and Intermediacy," *Journal of Comparative Administration* 2, no. 4 (February 1971): 407.

6. Katz and Danet, in their essay, "Making Organizations Work For People," suggest greater benefits from decentralization alone than Dr. Foster anticipated: "[I]f clients feel more efficacious vis-a-vis big organizations the deleterious effects of . . . bureaucracy may be reduced. Schemes for decentralization and . . . 'citizen participation' will by definition reduce the scale of big organizations, making face to face encounters in a more personal atmosphere posible. And controls . . . should not only obtain redress of grievances for the 'little man,' but ultimately improve the overall efficiency of service to the public." Elihu Katz and Brenda Danet, eds., *Bureaucracy and the Public: A Reader in Official-Client Relations* (New York: Basic Books, 1973), p. 393.

poor system retards it. And a poor educational system with rising
costs merely dramatized the presumed need for improved efficiency. In spite of Seidman's belief that "economy and efficiency are
demonstrably not the prime purposes of public administration,"[7] these two goals continue to be the principal criteria by
which the public assesses bureaucratic performance.

Any effort to change an organization is undertaken in the face
of constraints. The question for the organizational leader is to
discover the nature and sources of those constraints and to devise
ways to overcome them. Public involvement also gave the new
superintendent an opportunity to identify possible sources of
support and opposition to the changes which he planned to
introduce.[8] However, a permissive environment is a permanent
condition; thus, its support for change can be misleading. As
with presidents, like Woodrow Wilson for example, Foster

entered each of his executive positions at a time when reform was the
order of the day and with a substantial fund of good-will to draw
upon.[9]

But Alexander and Juliette George also pointed out that after
Wilson's initial successes with reform, he encountered "equally
impressive political deadlocks or setbacks later on."[10] Similarly,
Foster suffered setbacks after initial success, but they were less
dramatic than those of Wilson. And Foster's responses to his
setbacks were quite different from those of Wilson.[11] The issues of
success and response to setbacks are discussed in chapters 4

7. Harold Seidman, *Politics, Position and Power: The Dynamics of Federal
Organization* (New York: Oxford University Press, 1970), p. 27; see also the
observations of Jesse Bukhead on this view in *Government Budgeting* (New
York: Wiley, 1956), pp. 25-26.

8. Robert P. Biller, "Adaption Capacity and Organizational Development,"
in *Toward a New Public Administration: The Minnowbrook Perspective*, ed.
Frank Marini (Scranton, Pennsylvania: Chandler, 1971), p. 101. See also the
sources cited there, especially F. E. Emery and E. L. Trist. "The Casual Texture
of Organizational Environments," *Human Relations* 18, no. 1 (February 1965):
21-32. Trist and Emery discuss this issue in the context of a private organization
which was losing its customers due to a failure to adapt to technological
advances. The firm was unable to compete effectively against firms which
moved more rapidly.

9. Alexander George and Juliette George, *Woodrow Wilson and Colonel
House* (New York: Dover, 1964), p. 320.

10. Ibid.

11. See especially chapter 15 in George and George, *Woodrow Wilson and
Colonel House.*

through 6 in the context of specific analyses of efforts to change the structure of his organization.

In the narrow sense of the term, organizational change implies only an alteration in the formal structure of the organization. If nothing more were required we should probably see fewer instances of failure to initiate change in formal institutions. But we know that organizations are also social systems with networks of informal social relations which an organization chart does little to explain. Yet it is this informal organization which often makes the diagnosis and cure of organizational ills such a formidable task. "[B]ut seldom," says V. O. Key, Jr., "is a bureaucracy agile enough to adapt itself to rapid change of social purposes without many accelerated retirements and judicious transfers from key positions."[12]

In some cases a simple change in personnel may be sufficient to produce the desired results. However, moving people around, or out for that matter, may still not produce the appropriate solution if the task is one which no one knows how to perform.

A further source of constraints is the political executive himself. For any leader, a belief system,[13] concept of office, style of leadership and previous learning singly or individually can limit and frustrate his efforts to initiate purposive actions. His belief system may contain elements which cause an executive to discount or disregard some issues if they are inconsistent with his private beliefs. This seems to be especially the case with those beliefs comprising what has been called the "operational code."[14] The "code" consists of those beliefs and values which serve to interpret experiences and perceptions and which give form to a leader's actions.

12. Key, "Politics and Administration," p. 161.

13. See Milton Rokeach, *Beliefs, Attitudes and Values* (San Francisco: Jossey-Bass, 1969), pp. 6-13; see also the discussion in his *The Open and Closed Mind* (New York: Basic Books, 1960), pp. 40-42.

14. An early attempt to apply this concept to leadership behavior is found in Nathan Leites, *The Operational Code of the Politburo* (New York: McGraw-Hill, 1951); Alexander George later extended Leites' formulations in his essay "The Operational Code: A Neglected Approach to the Study of Political Leaders and Decision Making," *International Studies Quarterly* 13, no. 2 (June 1969): 190-222. Robert Jervis discusses the related issue of event interpretation in his essay "Hypotheses on Misperception," *World Politics* 20, no. 3 (April 1968): 454-79. Jervis observed that "decision makers tend to fit incoming information into their existing theories and images. [These] play a large part in determining what they notice" (p. 455).

His concept of office also informs the conduct of a political executive. It helps him to determine the nature and scope of actions which he may appropriately undertake as the incumbent in an executive position. A narrow concept of office may lead a political executive to disregard opportunities to act decisively in support of his goals and objectives. The political executive may mistakenly assume that his concept of office is agreeable to those who employ him because the interviews preceding a job offer failed to closely examine the candidate in this area. Foster, for example, had to "interview" the board to determine if his concept of the superintendent's office was consistent with the board's view of what kinds of activities it would sanction as the school system sought to better relations with the environment and improve the educational quality of its students.

Superintendent Foster engaged in activities which we more commonly look for in elected political executives. That is, his concept of office was more like that of the political entrepreneur who seeks to develop strong executive coalitions in support of his policies and programs. Like these mayors, Foster wanted the freedom

to ascertain which of the interests and powerholders in the community, county, state and federal governments [could] become political resources, suppliers and allies on behalf of alternative goals and programs. Such a leader also benefits from being able to foresee those interests and groups likely to oppose different programs in varying degrees and with various instrumentalities.[15]

Professor George's formulation clearly requires that the responsible political executive hold the initiatives in determining necessary purposes and courses of action. As a political man in the superintendency, Foster quickly began to gain the initiative in order to

maximize the weight of his leadership for expediting social change . . . by reshaping the political process in some way. *Once in office, such political personalities make it the first order of business to recast political institutions by reinterpreting and expanding the functions of existing*

15. Alexander George, "Political Leadership and Social Change," *Daedalus* 47 (Fall 1968): 1200; for related discussions see Robert A. Dahl, *Who Governs?* (New Haven: Yale University Press, 1960); Thomas Murphy, *Political Entrepreneurs and the War on Poverty* (Lexington, Massachusetts: D. C. Heath, 1972); and Raymond Wolfinger, *The Politics of Progress* (Englewood Cliffs, N.J.: Prentice-Hall, 1974).

roles or by creating new ones that better fit their needs, political style, and aspirations.[16]

Foster performed this recasting through a reinterpretation of the proper relationship between his organization and its public and a redefinition of his own role as superintendent. He also created new roles within the organization (the regional associate superintendents) and moved his organization via decentralization more deeply into the social environment. In a similar way community participation, in the selection of principals or through the Master Plan Citizens Committee, helped to blur the distinction between that which was organizational and that which was outside its boundaries. Community involvement was the first step toward creating the conditions that would facilitate the introduction of additional changes within the organization. In turn, these changes (PPBS and decentralization) would strengthen the new relationships between the organization and its public. This was a critical point for Foster's attempt at institution-building. Its importance is indicated by Landau:

Once the conditions are created, begin to be utilized, and their implications recognized by others outside the traditional organizational boundaries exchanges [between the organization and its environment] can no longer be handled by sacred formulae . . . they have become problematical—open to hypothesis and experiment.[17]

Dr. Foster believed it was his responsibility to formulate the hypotheses, to design and conduct the experiments. In spite of the authoritarian quality implicit in such a conception of leadership, the superintendent thought of himself as a different type of urban political executive. Alexander George described the characteristics of the change-oriented leader in the following terms:

It seems unlikely, therefore, that the leadership needed to deal with contemporary problems of poverty, equality, and social change in American cities will be offered by astute politicians who are motivated only by an interest in the mechanics of power and in power for personal gain. Such a leader must possess, in addition, a "sense of direction" and an affinity for moving society forward. He must be interested in government, not merely in politics.[18]

16. George, "Political Leadership and Social Change," p. 1206. Emphasis added.
17. Landau, "Linkage, Coding and Intermediacy," p. 407.
18. George, "Political Leadership and Social Change," p. 1198. David McClelland has made a related point in the following terms: "One leads people by

While Superintendent Foster was not concerned about power for its sake alone, he recognized that control of his organization would be essential to the successful implementation of his innovations. Broad participation in goal-setting may be desirable, but Foster controlled the development of his goals. The inherent contradiction between the human relations approach he hoped to adopt and that which he believed was required at the outset of his administration led the new superintendent to make some costly errors. These mistakes contributed to the lack of success of his programs. Still, they were not the sole cause.

In the following pages I have attempted to present a more extensive analysis of the obstacles to innovations in public bureaucracies. The focus of this analysis is the political executive, because the agenda for change is his, and no matter what others may or may not contribute, should he fail, it tends to be viewed by the public as a personal failure. This agenda problem can be partially anticipated by the executive. When he knows what he wants to do, the political executive runs fewer risks of being forced to act on issues or programs developed by others, no matter how well-intentioned or even compatible with his own ideas and policy preferences.

Foster's goal was organizational change. He believed that his innovations would produce solutions to some of the major problems of urban public education which arose during the 1960s. The superintendent had a capacity and willingness to work hard to achieve that goal. He believed that despite acknowledged resource deficiencies his organization could be changed in fundamental ways. While many members of the public think that such changes, especially those which promise increased efficiency and economy, can be made at little cost, it is not expected that an organizational head should fall victim to such thinking. In addition, the analysis of Foster's experience suggests that bureaucracies have a limited capacity to absorb change, as its impacts are felt more and more directly by the structures of the institution.

helping to set their goals, by communicating them widely throughout the group, by taking initiative in formulating means of achieving the goals, and finally, by inspiring the members of the group to feel strong enough to work hard for those goals." David C. McClelland, "The Two Faces of Power," *Journal of International Affairs* 24, no. 1 (1970): 45; see also the works cited above in note no. 9 for similar observations on the requirements for leadership.

The case presented here also reveals that a "gap" in the knowledge of what is needed to produce desired outcomes may exacerbate that limitation. Finally, the fate of Foster's innovations cannot be separated from the man himself. Just as the fact that he was black played a part in his selection, so, too, did it become an added pressure in his job. Although it was never explicitly stated, Foster believed that his tenure was, in some way, a test of blacks' fitness for senior administrative posts in other urban political systems. This belief clearly influenced his selection of policies. Dr. Foster's innovations also suffered because he gave insufficient attention to the ways in which they interacted with each other. And by assigning a "linchpin function" to PPBS, its failure would weaken even the partial adoption of community involvement and decentralization. The experience of the Oakland school system indicates that changing organizations is more than the elimination of bureaucratic recalcitrance or the hierarchical distribution of authority.

For the superintendent, and for those who watched or tried to help him achieve his goals, the three years of his tenure taught some painful lessons about leadership and organization. These constitute the basis for much of the discussion which follows.

2

The Politics of Succession in the Oakland Public Schools

Black political activism in Oakland was but a part of the general activism in many of the nation's large black communities. In a broad sense, the range of activities in which blacks were involved can be viewed as attempts to increase their control of political resources. Much of the agitation of the middle and late 1960s was focused upon the processes of leadership succession in urban bureaucracies. Ad hoc clientele groups and their supporters frequently and vigorously raised questions challenging the belief that bureaucracies operated on the basis of "neutral competence." Specifically, blacks took the position that public organizations should be more racially representative if they were to serve a public interest in which minority group concerns would occupy a visible place. With non-whites contending for more political power, bureaucratic succession frequently became intertwined with the candidates' racial or ethnic representativeness. In a number of cities black attention to the issue of political succession was a product of the vigorous debate over community control of schools and community participation in organizational decision making.

Before 1968 such issues had not garnered widespread community interest in Oakland's non-white communities. In common with many large, urban school systems, however, the Oakland public schools had their share of educational problems.

High school students had sought a role in curriculum design, particularly for ethnic studies, as well as in the area of discipline. The teaching staff was also restive over salary questions and class sizes. Several times a strike was threatened, only to be called off at the last minute. And, of course, there were demands for more non-white teachers in the district. But these problems had not assumed major proportion, in the opinion of most members of the Board of Education.

Thus when superintendent of schools Stuart Phillips announced his resignation on 1 July 1968 it was a surprise to the board and the public. This decision was all the more surprising because his contract had another two years before expiration.[1] Board members did not, however, consider finding a replacement to be a serious problem. As far as they were concerned, it would simply be a matter of announcing the vacancy and selecting the best qualified individual from those who would apply.

HOW MUCH TIME IS ENOUGH?

In the belief that this task could be set aside until after the schools opened in the fall, the board took no immediate steps to seek a new chief administrator. In any event Dr. Phillips' resignation was to be effective on 1 July 1969; surely nine months would be more than enough time.

By December 1968 the Board of Education was ready to name the members of the screening committee which would assist them in finding a new superintendent. The board proudly announced that it had spent considerable time in listening to a variety of community organizations and individuals express their views on the qualities desired in the new man. The Oakland Black Caucus, which had achieved some political successes in other arenas of the city's politics (notably in OEO and Model Cities projects), sought an *organizational* role in either screening or selecting candidates. However, Oakland's board members turned the demands aside. One member of the board saw the Black Caucus' interpretation of "community participation" to mean that "they

1. This resignation was not, however, entirely voluntary. A coalition of liberal and conservative elements in the city had worked carefully and discreetly to secure it. In general the reason given for wanting a new man in the top schools job was the inability of the system to cope with environmental changes under the incumbent's leadership.

not only wanted to participate—they actually wanted to name the superintendent! The Board couldn't abrogate their responsibilities."

This interpretation of the caucus' demand allowed the board to justify their refusal on the grounds that the caucus did not represent "the public interest."[2] Moreover, the presence of two blacks on the seven-member Board of Education, and the fact that each member was elected at large, helped to sustain the board's collective belief that it did represent the community's interest.[3] To them, the selection of a new superintendent was an important, but nevertheless routine task; community participation had been satisfied by listening to individuals during formal board meetings and through informal conversation with community members.

As a formally independent governing unit, the Board of Education was removed from the mainstream of city politics. Developments in other issue areas, for example the black effort to gain control of OEO programs, was not part of their decision context. The perceptual constraints which resulted from this limitation formed the basis for much of the conflict between the school board and the most attentive members of its public as the search for a superintendent progressed.[4]

The selection of a new school superintendent in a medium-sized American city does not immediately raise questions which command the attention of very many people. Political considerations might arise if the appointment were to be made by a mayor

2. Just how we can discover this interest is the subject of considerable debate. See Walter Lippmann, *Essays in the Public Philosophy* (Boston: Little, Brown, 1955); Emmette S. Redford, "The Never-Ending Search for the Public Interest," in *Ideals and Practice in Public Administration*, ed. Emmette S. Redford (Tuscaloosa, Ala.: University of Alabama Press, 1958), pp. 107-37.

3. The caucus tried but was unsuccessful in attempting to show that, with two exceptions, all of the board had initially been appointed and had subsequently run as an incumbent. This is a characteristic of electoral politics in many "reform" cities such as Oakland. The normal advantages of incumbency are further strengthened by non-partisanship. Eugene Lee provides an excellent analysis of these and other issues in his *The Politics of Non-Partisanship* (Berkeley: University of California Press, 1960); see also Oliver Williams and Charles Adrian, "The Insulation of Local Politics Under the Nonpartisan Ballot," *The American Political Science Review 53*, no. 4 (1959): 1052-63.

4. See the discussion of this concept in Aaron Wildavsky, "The Analysis of Issue-Contexts in the Study of Decision-Making," *Journal of Politics* 24 (November 1962): 717-32.

or if there were other obviously partisan political overtones to the process. Neither of these conditions existed in Oakland in early 1969 as the search for candidates got under way.

Had the board used the available literature on leadership selection, they would have been no better prepared for what was to come. Some years ago Marshall Dimock and Howard Hyde set forth their idea of the requirements for executive leadership in bureaucracy. They proposed that

The executive not be too old upon appointment; that he remain in office long enough to be effective but not so long as to become senile; and that positions of leadership be attractive to potential leaders.[5]

If these were the only rules guiding selection, there would be little reason to examine executive succession in bureaucracies. Indeed, it is just this kind of apolitical prescription which appears to have limited investigations of the issue.

Perhaps because his work dealt principally with the problems of succession at lower echelons of private organizations, Oscar Grusky's research has failed to attract the attention of political scientists. Yet his work produced at least two observations which have implications for the organizational processes of public bureaucracies. "Succession is important for two basic reasons," Grusky stated. "It always leads to organizational instability, and it is a phenomenon that all organizations must cope with."[6] Nevertheless most formal organizations can tolerate some degree of succession-induced instability, as Stanley Davis reminds us: "Although the problems of succession . . . can create strains in an organization's structure, it [sic] seldom is severe enough to destroy that structure."[7] And Oakland's school board members wanted to minimize the anticipated "strains" as much as possible.

ALTER THE ROUTINES OF SUCCESSION: DON'T CONSIDER INSIDERS

When the Board of Education began to look for a new superintendent, a number of observers expected the post to go to one of

5. Marshall E. Dimock and Howard K. Hyde, "Executive Appointment in Private and Public Bureaucracies," in *Reader in Bureaucracy*, ed. Robert K. Merton et al. (Glencoe, Ill.: Free Press, 1952), pp. 319-20.

6. Oscar Grusky, "Administrative Succession in Formal Organizations," *Social Forces* 59, no. 2 (December 1960): 105.

7. Stanley M. Davis, "Entrepreneurial Succession," *Administrative Science Quarterly* 13, no. 3 (1968): 403.

its current senior staff. The board could have made a choice among the three assistant superintendents (one of whom was black) or the business manager, who had almost forty years' experience in the district. Such promotions from within are said to assure continuity in the organization's activities.[8] Still, continuity may be an obstacle to the achievement of other objectives. The members of the school board had made up their minds that the system needed to be changed. With the power to appoint resting with them, it was only natural that they would look to change at the political executive level. Moreover, the appointment could also be interpreted by interested members of the public as a statement of educational policy for the school district. Despite their belief that the school system was not political, the board members saw an opportunity to break with past practices in choosing a replacement for Dr. Phillips. They may not have viewed their decision to exclude insiders from consideration as "political," but it certainly implies a degree of political awareness.

In part, Oakland's current staff were not considered because they were too specialized.[9] That is, the professional socialization of these men had taken place exclusively within the Oakland schools. And they were all closely identified with the practices— many of which they had helped to formulate—of that single system. Moreover, their narrow base of professional experience suggested that these applicants were likely to be closely linked to existing staff members and would be vulnerable to the pressures of loyalty and obligation. Indeed, one board member bluntly stated his belief that "the old guard couldn't handle the situation." As in Gouldner's study of managerial succession, the board expected that its new political executive would be "able to view the situation in a comparatively dispassionate light and [be] freer to put his judgments into practice."[10] It was, thus, a combination of concerns which persuaded the Board of Education to look

8. In this connection see the discussion of the adverse consequences of promoting from within in Alvin Gouldner, *Patterns of Industrial Bureaucracy* (Glencoe, Illinois: The Free Press, 1954). The fact that most of the other administrative staff of the system (principals, supervisors, directors) had been trained and promoted by these men made this an especially difficult issue.

9. However, the Board of Education did not announce this decision publicly. In fact, several of Oakland's senior staff did submit applications.

10. Gouldner, *Patterns of Industrial Bureaucracy*, pp. 71-72.

beyond the system for a new superintendent of schools.[11] However for the Oakland public schools "going outside" was not to ensure a smooth transition of leadership.

The "situation" to which the board member quoted above referred was a euphemism for the substantial change in the racial composition of the student body. In keeping with national trends, the proportion of white students in the Oakland schools had declined steadily during the 1960s. By the time of this study whites constituted barely 25 percent. And as might be expected, black students comprised more than half of the total student body. The evidence from other school systems notwithstanding, Oakland's school officials saw no portent of political conflict in this change. To the extent that race was considered at all by administrators or the board, it was almost solely in terms of learning. Low achievement scores for a substantial part of the black student body was not a political matter.

As we have since learned, there is a considerable risk to this kind of issue simplification. Of course, school boards are not alone in narrowly defining the problems to which they must attend. Wildavsky found that members of Congress similarly constrained their perceptions of issues. Quite naturally, individuals cannot consider every piece of relevant information when reaching a decision. But to narrowly construe an issue out of habit rather than careful deliberation can lead those with the responsibility for decisions to define the situation in accordance with their stereotypes and drastically restrict consideration of alternatives and consequences. As Wildavsky observed,

A stimulus [low achievement scores on standardized tests among blacks] may be treated as belonging to a well-known type [high absenteeism or poor study skills] because of some partially perceived surface characteristics, thus invoking the standard responses [truancy prevention or more study halls], when it actually contains novel features requiring . . . different kinds of actions.[12]

The board steadfastly refused to acknowledge the legitimacy or relevance of an interest which did not come from one of the traditional school-related interest groups, such as the PTA. The

11. One board member recalled, however, that several former insiders were seriously considered *until* community pressure became very strong. Among these candidates was a black state official who had formerly been an Oakland principal.

12. Wildavsky, "The Analysis of Issue-Contexts," p. 718.

board members did not understand, or could not recognize, the differences in the social environment of the school system. It was still business, more or less, as usual.

Because board members knew they had other crucial tasks before them (e.g., preparing for a tax election and the district's budget), they retained the services of a consultant panel to help find a superintendent.[13] In the belief that the makeup of the consultant group would reinforce their attempt to depict the process as being open and fair, the board was careful to see that the screening committee was racially balanced.[14] In addition, the board committed itself (or allowed the impression to spread that it had committed itself) to interviewing no candidate who had not come through the screening process.

Once the consultant panel began its work in January 1969, the board turned its attention to other matters.[15] The board expected little difficulty in filling the post. In any event, screening was a time-consuming task, and board members and the outgoing superintendent were more interested in the preparations for the spring tax election. The public's attention was also directed to other school matters. Organized groups such as the PTA and the League of Women Voters were working with the board and administration in support of the tax increase. Teachers, who might have been expected to show some interest in selecting a new school executive, were more concerned about the potential loss of 100 teaching positions and cutting one class period from the school day.

The black community was also engaged elsewhere. The Black Caucus was struggling with Oakland officials for control of the local anti-poverty program and the allocation of Model Cities

13. An article in the *American School Board Journal* 158 (April 1971): 35-36, refers to the "traditional consultant-panel" method of selecting school superintendents. See Carroll F. Johnson, "How to Pick a New Superintendent and Shine Up Your Public Image While You're at It."

14. There were two black and two white consultants. The white members were professors of education from the University of California and Stanford University. One of the black members was an assistant vice chancellor from the University of California at Berkeley while the other was head of the United Negro College Fund.

15. In addition to preparing the school budget for the coming year, a process that requires about six months, several board members would be campaigning for reelection in the spring of 1969. This may also have diverted some of their attention from filling the superintendency.

funds. Moreover, the work of the consultant panel and the board was not in public view because the selection of a new superintendent was a personnel matter which the board handled in executive session. Thus, the search for a new superintendent was initially given little attention by the board and potentially interested members of the public due to what appeared to be more pressing, immediate issues.

WHAT KIND OF MAN DID THE
OAKLAND PUBLIC SCHOOLS WANT?

Despite their withdrawal from active screening the board members had a good idea of the qualifications they wanted in a new chief executive.[16] The board did not indicate a preference for courses in education. Nor did they ask for applicants with a specific degree. Instead, and somewhat surprisingly to some, they preferred applicants whose training showed an "emphasis on the liberal arts or humanities."

Like a number of school districts, Oakland was beginning to think that traditional training in educational administration did not provide the managerial skills which were needed to run a complex organization. Of importance to the applicants, however, were the stipulations with regard to administrative experience.

Oakland specifically required an individual with "successful administrative experience in urban school districts." They believed that the applicant should show "breadth and variety in level and extent of authority for independent action. There must be experience and familiarity with . . . problems in a metropolitan community of heterogeneous socioeconomic and racial composition." Specifically, the board sought an individual who had "demonstrated the ability to obtain the respect of the community, to secure its cooperation and to *support* it in its efforts to improve the quality of Oakland's educational opportunities."[17] In Oak-

16. Except where otherwise indicated, the discussion of qualifications is based on the brochure "Oakland Looks Ahead: The Search for a *New Superintendent*" [emphasis in original], The Board of Education, Oakland Unified School District, n.d. This document was prepared in the summer of 1969 but was based upon criteria developed in the winter of 1968-69.

17. In the preliminary statement the word *support* did not appear. Originally the board had used the term *lead*. This change was made to reflect some concern for the community participation interests. An indication of the importance attached to the ability to work with the community can be gained by noting that it is mentioned specifically under three of the seven desired qualifications.

land, as in most large urban school systems of the late 1960s, "community" meant non-whites in general and blacks in particular. The board's brochure stated that "a record of involvement with minorities will be very essential." This last requirement clearly reflected some concern with the demands of the black community in Oakland. And it should have been recognized as a requirement for political skill. But as I indicated earlier, the board could not conceive of public education as in any way related to politics.

The Board of Education wanted a lot from a new superintendent. Not only did they want his ability as an educational leader recognized at the local level, they also expected him to possess "recognition . . . in the large body of the profession." They obviously sought someone with national stature.

"Leadership, as conceived here," the board said, "includes skill in oral and written communication and ability in public relations."[18] The leader of the Oakland public schools was expected to have "the qualities of the educational statesman: courage, foresight, integrity, [and] willingness to fight for what he believes to be right." These qualities imply a set of activities which the board members considered the appropriate responsibilities of administration. Perhaps the only qualification not included was the ability to walk across the man-made lake on his way to the district's offices.

In the specification of what it wanted in the way of leadership, the board also created a potential obstacle to its successful exercise. In keeping with much of the prescriptive city management literature which emerged in the early twentieth century, Oakland's board members thought in terms of the presumed dichotomy between administration and policy:

[The board] expects to establish policy and then to allow the superintendent freedom to carry out the policies. The members of the board expect the superintendent to carry the administrative duties of the school district.

18. This may strike some readers as a small matter, inappropriate for a brochure soliciting applicants for a high-level administrative post, but the Oakland public schools system had once been embarrassed by a letter full of grammatical and spelling errors written to the editor of a local paper by one of its principals.

Despite ample evidence to the contrary, many elected officials in medium-sized "reform" cities also continue to hold to a belief in the non-political character of the duties of an appointed political executive. As we will see in the Oakland school board's case with Marcus Foster, however, the policy-administration division and the non-political ideal seem to have been no more than nods to a managerial fiction.

THE PANEL AND THE BOARD GET TO WORK

After approving the search procedures, the board turned its attention and efforts to other school business and left the consultants to begin the screening process. In late January 1969 the president of the board announced that a new superintendent would probably be named in March. The announcement of the Oakland vacancy had been given wide distribution, and from the sixty applications received by the screening committee the board believed they could easily find a suitable candidate. The consultant panel soon completed its work, reducing the larger group to about a dozen men who were brought to Oakland for personal interviews. The panel was then disbanded.

Although the board had wanted to consider some black applicants for the post, the first offers went to whites. Later one of the black members of the board observed that the small number of black applicants resulted from poor use of the consultants. It was unrealistic, however, to expect many blacks to apply, because there were few blacks in senior educational positions around the country. There was, in addition, a further problem with the few blacks who did submit applications. Most of them were from California and were known in one capacity or another to either members of the board or the administration. Familiarity did not work to their advantage (nor did it help the white applicants from California).

The promised announcement did not come in March because neither of the two men to whom the post was offered would accept. In making these selections, the board was forced to make some compromises with the criteria they had established. Their first choice was from a medium-sized city in New England with a student enrollment of approximately 20,000, less than one-third the size of Oakland.[19] This man had the general background that

19. Oakland was looking for the professional advisor type of superintendent

Oakland wanted in terms of educational training and experience, but he lacked the involvement with a racially and socioeconomically diverse community. However, he was acceptable because the members of the board believed that he had the intuitive judgment to cope with the problems of the Oakland schools. He refused the offer without elaboration. The second choice was from the Northwest and had at one time been employed by Oakland. But by the time the board made its offer he was no longer interested.

The board was now facing a dilemma. They had neither a new superintendent, nor the consultant panel to help them in their search. This dilemma was made worse by an expectant and concerned community which had been promised a man to fill the post. Moreover, time now became an issue in the selection process because the tax election deadline was drawing closer. A full-time superintendent was believed necessary because he is the manager of such campaigns. Although the outgoing executive was still in office, it was thought that his successor should have the major responsibility in this effort because projected revenues would be a major part of future educational planning. The board decided that they had to act. After all, naming a successor to Superintendent Phillips was *their* responsibility, with or without consultant help.

THE BOARD GOES IT ALONE

The board members were depressed and anxious. They could have reactivated the screening panel, but because time was short they decided to go it alone. A man who had been considered for superintendency some years before was contacted, but he was no longer interested in the Oakland job. He did, however, suggest the name of "an exciting young superintendent from Las Vegas, Nevada, as a man the board ought to talk to."[20] The board followed through on this recommendation. On April 26 the directors

---

described by Ramsey and McCarty, but these authors also point out that the "skilled educational practitioners are not found in the big urban complexes or in rural villages . . . they are more likely to be discovered in suburban light-house districts." Donald J. McCarty and Charles E. Ramsey, *The School Managers* (Westport, Conn.: Greenwood Publ. Corp., 1971), p. 144.

20. The board's anxiety was related to the prospects for passage of the tax increase in June 1969 if a new superintendent were not selected by that

of the board interviewed Dr. James J. Mason for about six hours. Late in the afternoon of that same day he was offered the job; four days later he telephoned his acceptance.

The board made no public announcement of this offer.[21] Indeed, the Oakland public was completely unaware of these developments. They learned of the school board's negotiations with Dr. Mason from a story in the *San Francisco Sunday Examiner & Chronicle*. A reporter had pried the information loose in Las Vegas, Nevada, where Mason was then superintendent of the Clark County schools. But no matter, thought the board; this was simply an enterprising journalist's scoop of the home town paper. They believed they had solved one of their biggest problems and could now get on with other important business. As it turned out, the board's method of selecting the new superintendent had set in motion a chain of events which proved to have high political costs, among other things spelling defeat for the much-needed tax rate increase.

"HASTE MAKES WASTE"

That the board's negotiations with Dr. Mason were held in closed session was acceptable to most people in Oakland because it was a legitimate personnel matter.[22] However, the press disclosed that the new superintendent was chosen without the help of the "blue ribbon screening committee" (the consultant panel); a number of Oakland citizens believed the board had violated the community's trust. The consultants, after all, had been depicted by the board as surrogates for direct community involvement. It is possible that the Board of Education could have weathered even this controversy had it not also been for an additional piece of information which came to light on the Tuesday following the initial announcement of the offer. Again the news came from the *San Francisco Chronicle*: a taxpayers' group in Las Vegas had charged

---

time. The head of a tax-supported agency often plays a critical role in efforts of this type. *Montclarion*, 14 May 1969.

21. Perhaps they were simply holding the announcement until Dr. Mason formally accepted; he had to get a release from his contract with Las Vegas before doing so. The problem about the release was Oakland's need to have a superintendent on board in time to help secure the passage of the tax increase.

22. The *Montclarion* suggested that the Board of Education was "hiding" behind the provisions of the Brown Act, which permits public bodies to discuss personnel questions in executive sessions.

Oakland's superintendent-designate with a conflict of interest, stemming from an honorarium paid to him by a publishing firm which subsequently received a $1 million textbook order from his school district. This charge gave an already disturbed community "proof" that the Board of Education had mishandled their job of selecting the school system's chief executive. In their haste, the board members had failed to make even a cursory background check on their "handpicked" superintendent.

At its meeting the following week, the Board of Education was confronted by a capacity audience. Spokesmen for the Oakland Black Caucus were the most overtly hostile, but there was a general sense of confusion and anger throughout the audience. For the most part the audience wanted to know why the board had not followed its own procedures. The board president was evasive in responding when the question was directly put to him by a high school student: "Why wasn't the process followed? It's a simple question. . . ."

When [board president Lorenzo] Hoopes did not answer immediately, the audience shouted: Answer the question! Answer the question! Hoopes then stated: The board followed the procedure to the extent it was possible to do so. This was met with groans from the audience.[23]

The answer was clearly not satisfactory. But then the audience got the answer it wanted from an unexpected source. One of the Black Caucus representatives in the audience bluntly asserted,

Mason is not going to be the new superintendent. I saw Billingsley [Andrew Billingsley, one of the two black members of the first screening committee] the other day and he told me he had never heard of Mason.[24]

The revelation that the consultants knew nothing about the new superintendent stunned the audience. The broad support for the much sought-after tax hike was put in direct jeopardy when several white speakers from the more affluent "hills" area of Oakland spoke. The League of Women Voters' president told the board:

Recent events have raised . . . serious questions which must be answered fully and clearly before voters go to the polls in June. Last month the league decided to support the proposed $1.95 increase, but recent confusion has caused the league to pause.[25]

23. *Montclarion*, 28 May 1969.   25. Ibid.
24. Ibid.

A president of a local PTA group told the board she was totally frustrated by the board's action in her efforts to support the tax increase and the Oakland schools. "How can I go out and ring doorbells . . . when there is no trust in the Oakland board of education?" She said her friends reacted to Dr. Mason's appointment by laughing loudly and saying, "Well, Oakland has done it again!"[26]

This last remark was quite similar to the view of the Black Caucus that they could always expect the worst from the Board of Education. The events in "l'affaire Mason" appeared to many to have confirmed the caucus' suspicions. The board's troubles with this appointment also gave the caucus a chance to achieve further political gains in the city. Exploiting an opponent's discomfiture is a time-honored practice.

Conditions at the board meeting deteriorated rapidly. Several groups demanded that the board rescind its decision to hire Dr. Mason, saying they would stay until the board complied. The board refused. A number of protesters blocked the main doors to the board room, which the board interpreted as a threat to keep them inside. The police were called, and a scuffle between them and some of the protesters erupted. The scuffle was brief but resulted in the arrest of the president of the Oakland Federation of Teachers, several members of the caucus and a high school student leader. The president of the local NAACP chapter (also a member of the caucus) helped to keep things from getting worse by leaping on a table and persuading the audience to "cool it." In spite of the brevity of the episode and the minimal level of physical conflict, the damage to the images of the board and the Oakland public schools was done. An event such as this was sure to get broad media coverage, and it certainly did make front-page news in the Bay Area press. A spectacle of violence at the school board meeting caused many more people in the community to become aware of the schools' problems. People who might have been inclined to support the board could not help but be influenced by what had happened at this meeting. As far as the tax election was concerned, black supporters now became active opponents.

26. Ibid.

LOSING WITHOUT REALLY TRYING

There is ample evidence that urban revenue measures draw some of their most stable support from non-white citizens.[27] And in view of the traditionally low turnout at local elections and the usual requirement for a two-thirds majority on such revenue issues, the Oakland schools could not afford to lose black supporters. Furthermore, the public schools did not have a good record of gaining public support for the school system's revenue needs, as we can see from Table 1.

To compound their political problems, the board also lost the support of another key group when the head of the teachers' union was arrested: organized labor withdrew its support. The lone liberal member of the board tried to get his colleagues not to press charges, but they refused. In the long run, the board might have been hurt more if they had dropped the charges, because a substantial portion of the Oakland public was incensed over the tactics of the caucus in particular. The Black Caucus, however, had been given an issue which could be put to political use. In addition, they found an attentive constituency among the teaching staff. The arrested leaders had become political symbols with which to harangue the school officials. And the resulting trial assured the critics of press attention, thus furthering the erosion of public support for Oakland's educational system.

It cost the Oakland public schools almost $7,000, including the travel expenses for the other job candidates, to find Dr. James Mason. In the context of an annual budget of $55 million, this is a small sum. But how does one calculate the political cost incurred as a result of the board's errors in judgment? The loss of the tax election was almost certainly attributable to the active opposition of former supporters of the measure. The resulting revenue loss to the schools was in the millions, and the educational program suffered further weakening. Undoubtedly, the board's credibility was also damaged by its temporizing on the public's questions about the selection process. In their haste to act on

27. The value of black support on such local finance questions has been examined in James Q. Wilson and Edward C. Banfield in their "Public Regardingness as a Value Premise in Voting Behavior," *American Political Science Review* 58 (December 1964): 876-87. For some modifications of their judgments on "ethos," see also their "Political Ethos Revisited," *American Political Science Review* 65 (December 1971): 1048-62.

their conception of statutory duties, these elected officials had broken a pledge to the Oakland public.

The consequences of that breach of community trust were exacerbated by changes in the school system's political environment which the board either misunderstood or failed to see. That is, the black constituency and clientele groups of the public schools had become more assertive in Oakland, as in other large urban school systems. Obviously the board members knew that changes were taking place; otherwise they were not likely to have developed the list of qualifications for the new superintendent as they did.[28] In particular the several references to "working with the community" and ability to deal with educational problems in a multiracial system clearly indicated such awareness. Nor was it the case that protest was unknown in Oakland. Throughout much of this period other parts of the city government were involved in community conflicts concerned with control of the poverty program, "police brutality," and other issues. The Board of Education nonetheless persisted in believing that the schools were somehow insulated from those controversies. As a "purely" personnel matter, naming a new superintendent raised no substantive questions of public interest—or so it was thought. How did it happen that this "little group of neighbors"[29] could so thoroughly antagonize the constituents whose interests they were elected to represent?

THE SCHOOL DIRECTORS AS "A LITTLE GROUP OF NEIGHBORS"

In part an answer to the question just posed can be derived from the concepts of office which board members held. In their collective self-concept the school directors[30] believed themselves to be representatives of a unitary community interest in good government. The board tried to act in ways which would reinforce the view that they were serving that interest.

The members of the board might claim to represent the public's interest, but were they representative of that public? As is

28. See the discussion of adaptability in Burton R. Clark, "Organizational Adaptation and Precarious Values: A Case Study," *American Sociological Review* 21 (June 1956): 327-36.

29. This phrase is taken from James W. Davis, Jr. and Kenneth M. Dolbeare, *Little Groups of Neighbors* (Chicago: Markham, 1968).

30. Members of the school board have the formal title of "director."

TABLE 1: The Oakland Schools' Record of Public Support on Revenue Measures

Bond or tax issue	% Favoring issue	% Turnout	Opposition arguments
June 1952 School Tax	48.9	43.9	Schools have overestimated their expenditures — as they regularly do — and underestimated their revenues. In addition, new state aid is very likely.
March 1954 School Bonds: Earthquake Proofing, New Construction	62.6 61.4	23.4 22.9	Amount requested is excessive, and the school board has not been candid about the uses of the money; there is a lack of planning and no
School Tax	39.3	22.1	need to rush into the bond issue and a special election.
June 1954 School Bonds: Earthquake Proofing, New Construction	60.1	33.6	
June 1956 School Bonds	73.5	44.5	
February 1958 School Tax	44.8	21.7	No urgent need for school money; it will only go into salary increases for teachers; a tax increase of about $.70, expiring in 5 years, and used only for backlog of maintenance and equipment is justified.

Bond or tax issue	% Favoring issue	% Turnout	Opposition arguments
June 1958 School Tax	50.8	43.7	Increase is excessive; it should be only about 2/3 of the proposed increase.
May 1965 School Tax	18.9	28.3	Tax increase would push rates up too high; budget waste; salary increases not enough.
June 1966 School Tax	39.7	41.2	Same issue defeated last year; "goes far beyond meeting essential needs"; new state and federal funds will be available.
November 1966 School Tax	38.6	48.7	Lack of economy in schools; use of overrides to subvert voters' wishes; dehydrated version of proposal defeated before.
June 1969	32.5	34.7	School board unresponsive to blacks; schools already have sufficient funds.
June 1970	46.0	49.8	Broken promises and lack of priorities.

usually the case with such questions, the answer was equivocal. Oakland's school board had seven members, two of whom were black and one a woman. It was composed of residents with sound professional and business credentials and middle- to upper-status occupations: two attorneys, a senior vice-president of a national grocery chain, a local vice-president of a national brokerage house, the manager of a large auto and truck leasing firm, the co-owner of a small industrial corporation, and an executive in the regional office of a federal agency with experience as an accountant in Oakland's corporate community. This was a solidly middle-class group, and all were long-time residents of the city. With one exception they had served together for at least five years. (The exception was the stockbroker, who was elected in May 1971. He was also the son of a former board member.)[31] In terms of occupations or professions, then, the board's makeup was clearly not representative of a diverse urban community.

However, the board may possibly be representative functionally, if not socioeconomically. As a board member's service lengthens he/she becomes a representative of a particular community group by virtue of the development of a specialty, giving closer attention to some particular aspect of the school program than to others.[32] In practically all cases, some group of constituents either inside or outside the system already exists corresponding to each such specialty, who expect the board member to act as *their* representative.[33] An illustration of this point was provided by one of the black board members. While he denied being a captive of black interests in the city, this school director

31. In non-partisan political systems the "taboo" against businessmen entering political contests is less restrictive than seems to be the case in partisan environments. See the discussion of the origins of this taboo in the essay by Peter and Alice Rossi, "Some Historical Perspectives on the Functions of Local Politics," in *Social Change and Urban Politics,* ed. David Gordon (Englewood Cliffs, N.J.: Prentice-Hall, 1973), pp. 49-60.

32. The president of the Board of Education at the time the district's major troubles began was opposed to his colleagues developing specialties around any given area of the education program. According to his concept of boardsmanship, "we're better off not doing that very thing. . . . That's why there are no action committees . . . only study committees on the board." He went on to say, "Board decisions are by a committee of the whole . . . we don't want to have to rely on experts."

33. For another example of this *de facto* "representative function" see the discussion on the Presidium and the Secretariat of the CPSU in Zbigniew Brezinski and Samuel P. Huntington, *Political Power: USA/USSR* (New York: Viking Press, 1964), p. 162.

was quick to seize upon issues which had special significance to black students or the black community in general. For example, he gave close attention to having black businessmen compete for school contracts and construction awards. In addition he was a strong advocate of the use of vocational education and other special monies for the benefit of black and other non-white students. Not only did he become a de facto spokesman for black concerns, but his colleagues deferred to his judgment when such matters arose. The self-described liberal, and the only Democrat on the board, saw himself as the spokesman for liberal interests in the community. He was usually regarded as sympathetic by groups such as the Oakland Federation of Teachers (AFL-CIO) and minority interest groups, including the Oakland Black Caucus.

Functional representativeness notwithstanding, the board members believed themselves to be independent of any particular interest group. In part this was probably a natural consequence of at-large elections and the infrequent opposition to the incumbents.[34] One board member believed they were each independent of the electorate because their incomes did not depend on the schools. Such independence was thought to be desirable, for it allowed the board member to do what he or she thought was best. When the public disapproved of what a board member was doing, they could turn the offender out of office—"That's the way it's supposed to be."[35] In addition to this kind of indepen-

34. It is worth indicating that when Foster became superintendent he quickly discovered that the board members did have identifiable reference groups and constituencies. Thus the senior corporate executive is also seen as the spokesman for the major economic interests in the community as well as being the board's own expert on major purchases of equipment, e.g., computer hardware and the like. Small merchants and small businesses tend to look to the manager of the leasing firm for aid when they have matters for the board to consider.

35. This concept of representation resembles that held by members of Congress. See Lewis A. Dexter, *The Sociology and Politics of Congress* (Chicago: Rand McNally, 1969). Dexter's observation that "a congressman hears most often from those who agree with him" is especially relevant here. Also worth noting is his comment, "A Congressman's relationships with his district tend to be maintained through a small group of people he knew before he was elected" (p. 159). Wolfgang Pindar provides an interesting perspective on representation in the urban context in "The Urban Legislator: Problems and Perspectives," in *New Perspectives in State and Local Politics,* ed. James A. Reidel (Waltham, Mass.: Xerox Corp., 1971), pp. 227-45. For an extended discussion of representation see Hanna Pitkin's *The Concept of Representation* (Berkeley and Los Angeles: University of California Press, 1969).

dence, one former board member reported that "the school board was in contact with and was most frequently contacted by those people who had children in the public schools," but otherwise the board "was pretty much left alone to run the schools as it saw fit." In this sense, being left alone by the public reinforced the board's sense of independence and helped to promote a view of the public as being rather passive.[36]

INDEPENDENCE AND POLITICAL ISOLATION
EQUAL HELPLESSNESS

Oakland's Board of Education had only a limited conception of the public's interest in the selection of a new superintendent. The members of the board believed that they had an intuitive grasp of the city's educational problems as a result of long residence. "We pretty much know the general trend of the schools," claimed one member of the board. The board's information came from what they called "natural sources." "The board visits the schools. . . . Teachers, principals and the community get in touch with us. They alert the board to problems." However, these "natural sources" were a limited portion of the school district's total clientele. For board members were seldom in touch with the activist elements in the community. This was partly because the activists seldom had children in the schools; if one were not a parent, it was difficult to get the board majority's attention. Moreover, the activists' demands were not, in the opinion of these long-time officeholders, legitimate educational concerns. The Black Caucus was trying to make the schools a "political issue," and the board members believed that they had to protect public education from "politics."

Assistance of the consultants notwithstanding, the school board's ability to find and name a new superintendent was limited by factors which they could not control. To a considerable extent the board's difficulties were the result of a scarcity of time. They were, after all, serving only part-time, and the selection decision had to be reached during the school district's budget

36. This view of the public has also been described as the "subject orientation" in Gabriel A. Almond and Sidney Verba, *The Civic Culture* (Boston: Little, Brown, 1965), chapter 7, especially pp. 168-72. Also note their discussion of the kinds of problems which arise as citizens move into a "subject-participant" stance vis-a-vis their institutions (pp. 26-29).

process, a critical time in the school year. For the school directors, budget preparation afforded them their best opportunity to have a voice in educational policy, because budgeting is policy-making. Then, too, there was the impending tax election. With the outgoing superintendent playing only a small role in this campaign, the board members found themselves increasingly involved in small but time-consuming ways.

The Oakland school board could not silence its critics by giving in to public demands, nor were there any apparent bases for compromises. It could only suffer in silence the verbal attacks which followed the abrupt resignation of Dr. Mason.

THE BLACK CAUCUS TRIES TO EXPLOIT AN OPPORTUNITY

The members of the board still had not found a chief executive. But now they needed time to collect their thoughts and decide what to do next. And board members weren't the only ones who needed a respite from the recent controversies. The various public groups concerned with the schools, with the exception of the Oakland Black Caucus, also seemed relieved that at least one crisis had passed.

The caucus interpreted Mason's resignation and the defeat of the school tax hike as demonstrations of their political power. To some extent, of course, this was an accurate interpretation of recent events because caucus members had been the best organized and most vigorous critics of the board's handling of the selection process. In addition the caucus had considerable support from Oakland's teacher organizations, liberal citizen groups, and a large part of the student body. These were just as outspoken in their opposition, though perhaps less persistent. Emboldened by the taste of apparent victory, the caucus now escalated their demands. Where previously they had called for participation, the caucus now began to press for "a citizens' committee to design the procedure for selecting . . . a new superintendent. . . . The board was told to establish the committee to reflect the racial composition of the Oakland schools' population."[37] Few of the other critics followed the caucus' lead in this respect, for they too sought greater involvement in selecting the new superintendent.

37. *Montclarion*, 18 June 1969. This would have insured a black majority since blacks were more than 50 percent of the schools' enrollment.

However, according to press accounts, these groups lacked "confidence they [could] make a proper choice alone."[38]

For its part, the Board of Education continued to resist all demands for direct participation. Instead, the school directors sought to silence their critics by developing a new selection process. To help them with the task, the board again sought outside assistance. They turned to the California Association of School Administrators and the California School Boards' Association. Consultants from these two groups told the Oakland board members that community input was essential, that candor with the job applicants was imperative, and, finally, that they should retain several consultants to help with the search. In an oblique reference to the fact that the first coordinator of the search had been a former superintendent of the Oakland public schools, they also told the board that the search team should exclude Oakland public schools staff. None of these recommendations was particularly innovative, but because they tended to support the complaints made by Oakland residents, they were good public relations for the Board of Education.

This time the board selected a two-tiered arrangement for the consultant screening panel. They reactivated the original four-man group, but on top of this they placed a three-man team of "advisors" which would make final recommendations to the board. The chairman of the search group, a former school superintendent himself, had considerable experience in helping school districts find superintendents. In addition the advisors included a former superintendent of the Oakland public schools and Wilson Riles, a black state education official who was widely known and respected for his work in compensatory education.

To avoid charges of bad faith from the community, the chief advisor got the board's promise to make no moves to hire a superintendent without prior screening by the consultant panel. After quickly making that agreement public, the consultants immediately began to seek out community opinions. This was accomplished through meetings with groups and individuals around the city.[39] The consultants also designed a new announce-

38. Ibid.
39. A noteworthy exception was the Black Caucus. The board's consultants met with individual members of the caucus, but not with the entire group. They were criticized by some caucus members for employing what they saw as a divide-and-conquer strategy. Readers will recall that the group was quite

ment of the vacancy with a more systematic and professional statement of the qualifications for the post. This announcement candidly outlined the problems which would face a new superintendent in Oakland:

The problems confronting the board and the new superintendent as reported to us by [a] cross-section of community leadership are numerous, difficult of solution and far-reaching in their effect on the community. Major needs of the educational program require immediate attention. Conflicting interests and aspirations . . . as diverse as those voiced by the Black Caucus, The Alameda County Taxpayers Association, the organizations of teachers, and many others must be reconciled and united behind a positive program.[40]

In the background of these developments, however, the Black Caucus and the Oakland Federation of Teachers, the smaller and more activist of Oakland's teacher organizations, kept up a constant stream of criticism.

THE INFLUENCE OF THE
BLACK CAUCUS DECLINES

Throughout the summer of 1969 the Black Caucus continued its demands for direct community involvement in the selection process. In the minds of school officials these demands were understood to mean *caucus* participation. However, the Black Caucus was unable to maintain the broad support which it had enjoyed during the controversy leading to the resignation of Dr. Mason.

Several changes contributed to a weakening of the caucus' position. The Board of Education appeared to gain a sense of internal cohesion from the recent community conflicts. Instead of falling apart under caucus attacks, the board members drew closer together around the common cause of selecting a superintendent. And the new search and screening team was actively seeking out the opinions of several public groups on the kind of

---

successfully employed as a confrontationist device by a number of black organizations in the middle 1960s. For a lively account of how this tactic was used elsewhere see Tom Wolfe's essay, "Mau-Mauing the Flak Catcher," in his *Radical Chic* and *Mau-Mauing the Flak Catcher* (New York: Bantam Books, 1971). The advisory team and the screening committee reported that they had met with approximately 300 groups during the summer of 1969.

40. Several observers believe that the candid nature of this small booklet was helpful in establishing public confidence in the integrity of the selection process.

qualities Oakland's new superintendent should possess, and on the district's problems. The consultants also contributed to the erosion of the Black Caucus' support by conveying a sense of professional competence and political representativeness to established school-community groups. Moreover, once the consultants began their duties, public attention was diverted from the Board of Education.

While the caucus could no longer count on community-wide support, it remained a thorn in the side of the Board of Education. In October 1969 one of the caucus' co-chairmen told the board and the public, "All we're saying is we want final approval of the last four candidates."[41] But such statements no longer had much impact. The effort to acquire a decisive role in school politics was an extension of caucus activities in other political arenas of the city.[42] The organization sought to present itself as the embodiment of a unified black community's political aspirations in the city of Oakland. However, in the absence of broad support among the schools' public, and lacking the financial incentives contained in Model Cities or Community Action Programs, the caucus had little to offer prospective supporters. And, in the case of the schools, the board's consultants had preempted the caucus' principal issue, community involvement. Those who had been most attentive to the selection process were now willing to support the board's insistence on its exclusive right to name a new superintendent of schools.

THE BOARD SEARCHES FOR A UNANIMOUS VOTE

By mid-October the Board of Education had five recommendations from their consultants, but was unable to reach a unanimous decision on any of the five. Board members had agreed that they would not offer the job to a candidate who had less than unanimous board support. To do otherwise, they believed, would impose a handicap upon whomever they might select. The board recalled that its outgoing superintendent had been approved by a 5-2 vote, and they attributed some of the system's difficulties to this fact. Also, the future superintendent would be likely to interpret a simple majority vote as an indication of trouble

41. *Montclarion*, 1 October 1969.
42. See Judith V. May, "Two Model Cities: Negotiations in Oakland," *Politics and Society* 2:1 (Fall 1971): 57-88.

ahead. A unanimous selection would also let the schools' public know that the board was united despite its past difficulties.

By late October the Oakland Board of Education had made its unanimous selection and offered the post to a black educator from New Jersey. However, the board again failed to get the man of their choice. The circumstances surrounding this failure had nothing to do with community conflict. Indeed, the Black Caucus in meetings with the candidate had urged him to accept the post.[43] The Board of Education had scrupulously followed its procedures, a point which the board president stressed after learning that the offer had been refused: "We didn't make the mistakes we did with Dr. Mason. . . . We'll have to see what went wrong. . . . After all, he did come to California and was interviewed. He must have had some interest in the job."[44] Oakland's Board of Education had indeed made a mistake, although no one seemed to regard it as such at the time. They had breached an implicit code of ethics in recruitment: the offer to Dr. Ursell Watson of Trenton, New Jersey, was front page news in Oakland before he had personally informed his home district of the offer, much less his decision. The role which the untimely disclosure of the job offer played in Watson's decision to reject is not clear. Perhaps the involvement with Oakland served another purpose for Dr. Watson. It obviously gave him a stronger position from which to bargain with the Trenton board. We may also conclude that he was able to get the kind of commitment from them which would keep him in the New Jersey city.[45]

43. There were some in Oakland who believed that the caucus was attempting to dissuade Dr. Watson from accepting the post because it had not had a hand in his selection. The caucus maintained that it was only interested in giving a "brother" some "black input" which he could not get from other Oakland sources. *Oakland Tribune*, 28 October 1969.

44. Ibid.

45. In Trenton, New Jersey, where Dr. Watson was superintendent of schools, the school system was undergoing the same kind of stress that had characterized Oakland's schools. The *Oakland Tribune* reported on the response of Trenton to the job offer to its superintendent as follows: "News of Oakland's bid for Watson triggered a massive movement in Trenton with business, civic, racial and religious groups urging him to remain." According to the Trenton board president, "He has brought our community together. . . . He's brought about a spiritual renaissance in the schools" (*Oakland Tribune*, 28 October 1969). Some months later in a conversation with Marcus Foster, Watson told him that the salary increase (from $28,000 to $36,000) made it unnecessary for him to change jobs. But it should also be pointed out that Oakland's chief consultant in the search thought the incident of sufficient importance to prepare a subtly critical memo to board members on the protocol involved.

THE COURTING OF MARCUS FOSTER

Foster had learned of the Oakland vacancy from the large mailing of the first announcement. At that time (mid-1969), he simply was not interested in leaving his position with the Philadelphia schools and ignored it as he had done with similar announcements from other school districts.[46] However, Oakland contacted him directly through a telephone call from Dr. Harry MacPherson, the chief consultant to the Board of Education, who asked him to come out to Oakland for a job interview.[47] Foster was flattered but was still not sure that he was interested in the Oakland job. Shortly after the conversation with MacPherson, Barney Hilburn, a member of the Oakland board, contacted him. (Hilburn's wife had worked as a teacher under Foster in one of the Philadelphia schools.) Hilburn also asked him to come out to Oakland for an interview—"Just to take a look at it." Hilburn emphasized the need for a strong black educator in the city, a consideration which had some weight in Foster's own thinking. The combination of the call from MacPherson and the personal contact with a member of the board finally convinced Foster to come and look the situation over.

The weekend of his scheduled appointment in Oakland, Foster also had to make a consulting trip to the Dayton public

46. He had 23 years' service in the Philadelphia schools and would have had a sizable retirement income. In addition Foster believed he was likely to be a strong candidate for the top job in the Philadelphia schools in another five years. Foster's actions here suggest that Richard Carlson is correct in describing the two paths to the superintendency. Carlson observed that for schoolmen who want to be superintendent "two courses of action are open . . . one is to wait until the [position] comes to him, and the other is to seek a [position] wherever it can be found," Richard O. Carlson, *Executive Succession and Organizational Change* (Chicago: Midwest Admin. Center, University of Chicago, 1962), p. 7. I might add that the Oakland search process also revealed at least one example of the second path. One man applied twice for the job; the first time he could not make it through the screening committee. On his second application he got as far as the interview (with considerable help from a board member) but was then rejected by a vote of 7-0. He was subsequently hired by another large California school system where he lasted only two and one-half years on a four-year contract.

47. Just how Dr. MacPherson came to contact Foster is not clear. It is possible that he was suggested by Dr. Theodore Reller, a member of the screening committee who had been one of Foster's graduate instructors at the University of Pennsylvania.

schools.[48] On arriving in Dayton, he found that he was unexpected: his contact person had become ill and had failed to
notify anyone else of his impending arrival. In any case, when
Foster arrived at the Dayton high school to which he was assigned, he found himself in the midst of a student-instigated
crisis, with all of the student body out on the street threatening
horrible consequences if the district did not meet their demands.
As a result, most of Foster's "consulting" time that day was spent
in putting down the student disturbance and helping the students work out their grievances with the high school administration.[49] At the end of the day he "was just so damn beat" and still
somewhat ambivalent about the Oakland post that he called the
airport and cancelled his reservations for Oakland. He also tried
to cancel the Oakland visit. But the Board of Education was
persistent. Speaking for his colleagues, Hilburn assured Foster
that they would accommodate his need for rest by adjusting the
interview schedule. Again, Hilburn was persuasive: Foster came.

The meetings with the board left him with a good impression.
"The Board members asked good questions, hard but fair," he
said. What was more important to Foster, and probably to any
potential executive, was the board's expression of willingness to
follow a strong chief executive. Foster, the candidate, also asked
the board some hard questions of his own, principally to satisfy
himself that the board really wanted to get out of the business of
administration on a day-to-day basis. He came away with the
belief that the Board of Education wanted to have confidence in
the administration of the schools.[50]

48. This was under an arrangement established by a nationwide group of
black educators including Preston Wilcox, Rhody McCoy (both participants in
the Ocean Hill-Brownsville experiment) and Barbara Sizemore from Chicago,
Illinois. Unlike Foster, the other three were strong supporters of community
control, particularly New York's Ocean Hill-Brownsville experiment. Sizemore
subsequently became the first black woman to head a large urban school system
(Washington, D.C.). Her commitment to the ideology of community control led
to stormy conflicts with the District of Columbia Board of Education, ending
with her ouster.

49. It was this kind of leadership activity at Gratz High School which led to
Foster's national reputation as an educational leader.

50. Foster's questions in this area stemmed from the fact that the school board
had made an "acting" appointment after the Mason fiasco. It had meant,
however, that the individual board members found themselves involved in

On the plane back to Philadelphia Foster reflected on the interviews and discussions in Oakland. Although he believed he had handled himself well, he did not yet consider himself a serious candidate for the superintendency in Oakland. He weighed the Oakland potential against the good position he enjoyed in Philadelphia. Almost as soon as Foster got home, however, Oakland's chief consultant called to assure him that the Board of Education had virtually decided to offer him the job. Oakland wanted him, it seemed. But did Marcus Foster want Oakland?

Shortly after this conversation Foster flew to London to participate in an international conference on education, where he met Wilson Riles (who was not yet California's Superintendent of Schools). Riles knew of Foster's meetings with the Oakland public schools because he was part of the recruitment process.[51] The two black educators knew each other by reputation, but this conference was their first personal contact. Riles filled Foster in on the political environment of the Oakland public schools as well as giving him some insight into state and local relationships in California education.

Upon returning to Philadelphia from the London conference, Foster found that the chief consultant had called again. The Oakland Board of Education had cancelled all subsequent interviews pending some word from Foster. After receiving confirmation from the consultant that the Oakland Board of Education indeed wanted to disengage from administrative matters, Foster told his caller that he was interested. There was yet another trip to California, this time accompanied by his wife and this time including a round of dinners and informal social engagements with members of the Board of Education as well as members of the community. Two board members (one black, one white) were escorts during this visit.

After this second trip the board made its own on-site investigation of Marcus Foster. For this particular phase of the selection process they selected a colleague who had grown up in the

---

routine managerial aspects of the school district's affairs. Neither the board nor its acting superintendent found this arrangement satisfactory.

51. Wilson Riles had also been suggested as a possible candidate for the Oakland job early in 1969. His work as head of California's compensatory education program had given him a national reputation in public education.

Philadelphia area. Foster later said it couldn't have been better if he had planned it that way. Oakland's representative visited Philadelphia at a time when Foster was at the height of his popularity in the city. He had recently received Philadelphia's highest civic award, the Bok Prize. That award emphasized Foster's standing as a community leader. The strong, positive statements supporting Dr. Foster were decisive. The Board of Education had finally found the man to head the Oakland public schools.

WHAT DID OAKLAND GET?

The new superintendent of schools was impressive. The Board of Education was particularly happy that he had been a principal at all levels in Philadelphia, including some of the special discipline and adult schools. In addition, his most recent assignment as associate superintendent for community relations was viewed as perfect preparation for what the board members saw as a pressing need in Oakland. It did not matter that Marcus Foster had only 1½ years of administrative experience above the level of principal. For the board, this limitation was more than offset by his ability to "turn a school around," as his tenure as principal at Gratz High School demonstrated. For the new superintendent of the board, the value of the Gratz experience rested on the belief that a superintendent's most critical audience, at least initially, is found among the principals of a school district. Service at that level is usually a normal part of the preparation for higher offices in school administration. That Foster had been the principal of a "tough" high school, the board believed, would stand him in good stead with this important part of his staff. In its criteria for applications the board had also stated a preference for an individual with a doctorate. Certainly one could raise few objections to a wish to have the superintendent well-trained. A Ph.D. or Ed.D. would be an objective measure of such training. Foster did not have a doctorate, though at the time of his selection he was a candidate for a doctoral degree at the University of Pennsylvania.

But in the new superintendent's mind it was not enough to be a candidate for a degree. He viewed the lack of the "credential" as a potential handicap in dealing with the broader educational community. By the fall of 1970 Foster had received an honorary doctorate from a college in Pennsylvania. Possession of an honorary degree did not, of course, formally entitle Foster to be addressed as "Doctor." But this subtle distinction was lost on a good part of his public; and, while Foster did not encourage the usage, he did see an instrumental value in the assumption. It was indicative of the importance which style and form would assume in his leadership. Still, Superintendent Foster was aware that he was being a bit disingenuous. Consequently he spent some long nights during his first year in office completing his dissertation. His degree from the University of Pennsylvania was awarded in the following year.

Foster, like others who assume important posts, took pride in the fact that he did not seek the job; it sought him. The "courting" which I described earlier was an obvious boost to his self-esteem. In addition, his selection by Oakland's board enhanced the good reputation which had brought him to their attention in the first place. To the board members Foster was the educational statesman described by Richard Carlson. Such a man attempts

to move all phases of the educational program as far as he can. . . . He takes pride in the fact that he is never a candidate. . . . School boards come to him. . . . He is called a statesman because of the quality of his work and his concern for the long-run consequences of his acts for the whole educational program in the schools.[52]

In exchange for his acceptance, Foster, an outsider, was

given a mandate from the school board. The discussions preliminary to election are devoted to a give and take between outsider and the board. The board makes it clear that all is not well and that there is some interest in righting the situation. There is usually no specification of what needs to be done, but what is specified is . . . what the central problems are. By inference and by word, the outsider is given a mandate to act with respect to the problems. In giving a mandate to act . . . the school board assumes an obligation. . . . [It] signals a desire for a break with the old ways.[53]

While Carlson's use of the term "mandate" may be a little overdrawn, it was the board's commitment to change which helped Foster to make up his mind. Moreover, the school board selected its new political executive by a unanimous vote. This, too, was a commitment. It announced that the incoming executive would not have to contend with a divided governing board as he began his tasks. And as I pointed out earlier, the board

52. Carlson, *Executive Succession,* pp. 12-13.
53. Ibid., pp. 20-21.

members had agreed to allow Foster the maximum amount of discretion.

The selection of Marcus Foster as superintendent of schools was a departure from the traditional practices of the Oakland public schools. But as we can see from an examination of Table 2, Foster did not differ significantly from the others considered for the vacant post. He also resembled the majority of white superintendents around the country.[54]

It is interesting to observe, however, that Foster had more years of teaching experience than any of the other candidates. Presumptively, the full breadth of his educational experience gave him an advantage. It is at least worth speculating that were it not for race, Foster might have begun his administrative career earlier. In any event, the Black Caucus could argue, with some justification, that their demands had caused the board to search more widely than might otherwise have been the case. And as a result a fully qualified black person had been found for Oakland's top school post.

Perhaps, with equal justification, the Board of Education could claim that it had found the best-qualified person, who just happened to be black. It was now up to Foster to demonstrate his ability to do the job. The task of the political executive is difficult in the best of times. For Oakland's new superintendent of schools this difficulty was compounded by the generally unsettled nature of the system's political environment. Added to this was the uncertainty among board members, staff and community alike, based on Foster's race. What would a black superintendent do? As superintendent of schools Marcus A. Foster took every possible occasion to tell his public that what he intended doing was very simply to change urban education. That public could only wait to learn what he meant. The remainder of this study is an examination of the specific forms which change assumed under Foster's leadership.

54. On this point see the profile of school superintendents developed in the survey by Russell T. Gregg and Stephen J. Knezevich in "The Superintendent: What Makes Him What He Is," *American School Board Journal* 158 (June 1971): 16: "Close to one quarter . . . of superintendents taught for ten or more years before entering the field of school administration. And all of the superintendents serving in districts of 50,000 pupils or more had accumulated chalkdust on their sleeves for one or more years. So, in spite of the chatter about not restricting the choice of administrative candidates to those with teaching experience, school boards continue to favor superintendent nominees who possess an experience-based feel for what occurs in the classroom."

TABLE 2: How Foster Compared with Others Considered for the Job

Candidate	Age	Years of teaching experience	Years as principal or administrator excluding current post	Education	Present post	District size
I[a]	49	2	3	M.Ed.	Supt. 2 years	33,000
II[a]	37	3	V. prin. 1	Ed.D.	Supt. 2 years	5,000
III	49	3	None; bus. mgr. for 4	Ed.D.	Supt. 5 years	18,000
IV[a]	48	NA[b]	4	Ed.D.	Coordinator of Urban Education University	NA[b]
V	51	NA[b]	2	Ed.D.	Supt. 6 years	13,000
VI[a]	48	NA[b]	10	Ed.D.	Supt. 2 years	18,000
VII	45	2	2	Ph.D.	Supt. 3 years	20,000
Foster[a]	47	10+	5+	Ed.D. Cand.	Assoc. Supt. 1½ years	200,000+

[a]Black
[b]Not available

3

Shared Power and the Executive Constituency

Some leaders coming into an environment such as that surrounding the Oakland public schools in 1970 would understandably have moved with caution. Foster, however, seemed to think that caution would have been misinterpreted as indecisiveness or a lack of understanding. He had no intention of allowing misinterpretations to form or spread. As a result, the new superintendent did not view his situation as one in which he would learn to do his job: "I didn't come out here," he told one of his senior staff, "to learn how to be a superintendent. I had some notions about what I wanted!" There was little room to misunderstand the new superintendent's meaning. The implications of such statements have been made clear by many writers on leadership. F. G. Bailey has stated them well:

The man who correctly understands how a particular structure works can prevent it from working or make it work differently with much less effort than a man who does not know these things. . . . The man who understands the working of any organization or institution can find out which roles are crucial to the maintenance of those structures, and among these roles which are the most vulnerable.[1]

1. F. G. Bailey, *Stratagems and Spoils: A Social Anthropology of Politics* (New York: Schocken Books, 1969), p. 187. On this same point see the incisive essay on former Secretary of Defense McNamara in Eugene M. Zuckert, "The Service Secretary: Has He a Useful Role?," *Foreign Affairs* 44, no. 3 (April 1966): 463, 466-69.

Foster was just as certain that he also understood and could handle the school system's political problems. He believed in the necessity for public bureaucracies, especially big-city school systems, to find and develop ways to share power with their constituencies. While still in Philadelphia, Foster had begun to seek an answer to the question: "What is the appropriate relationship between a school and the surrounding community?" By the time he took office in Oakland, he could give an unequivocal answer:

There are some basic beliefs I have in what is necessary to deliver quality education . . . in urban settings. [O]ne of the basic principles, I think, that is essential in urban education is that there be broad based involvement in the educative process. I think that one of our difficulties across the country has been that we have not been skillful enough in involving people in the decision-making process.[2]

The sixties had provided an environment in which he could try to develop these skills. And his appointment as principal of Philadelphia's Gratz High School in 1968 had given him an opportunity to deal directly with questions of change. Before he could move in that direction, however, there were some immediate problems facing the new principal. Gratz was a difficult place for experimentation. The central administration viewed it as a tough, black school; and the Gratz community was critical of a stagnant, or worse, deteriorating school. Foster described the phenomenon in these terms:

In any kind of school setting, if the community believes nothing is happening, then, in fact, *for them* nothing is happening. There were some good things going on at Gratz . . . , but apparently the community was not aware of them.[3]

Because the situation was viewed in such a negative way Foster believed he had "to demonstrate very quickly to the Gratz community that it was a new day. [And] there was no available cushion for me to deal with careful planning for long-range change." Moreover, what the new principal would do was also of interest to a much broader audience. The Philadelphia Board of Education was attentive because of the criticism and publicity which attended Foster's appointment. In addition Philadelphia's

2. *Montclarion*, 14 April 1970.
3. Marcus A. Foster, *Making Schools Work: Strategies For Changing Education* (Philadelphia: The Westminster Press, 1971), p. 103.

black community had some interest because of a lengthy series by Philadelphia's black newspaper, the *Tribune,* that "took the school apart." The pressures to perform came, in part, from the outside, but Foster's desire to establish control over his organization (Gratz) was an added source of pressure.

In reflecting on the experiences at Gratz after leaving Philadelphia, Foster thought that the most important lessons were that it gave him "training with regard to survival, making decisions under crisis . . . hold[ing] a community together." But community for Foster had a particular meaning: it included the parents, teachers, and students of Gratz and, perhaps, the immediate environment of the school. He was trying to make the high school into a focal point for that "community's" concerns. "Holding the community together" was merely another way of saying that unified constituent and client support could fend off attempts by outsiders, for example college students, to exploit the unrest at Gratz. To counteract the threats he spent considerable time "pounding the pavement and knocking on doors" in an effort to persuade the Gratz community that legitimate educational concerns would be distorted or forgotten if they allowed their attention and efforts to be diverted by "outsiders." And he reminded the community that as a group they had won a victory over "the system" in the struggle for the gymnasium addition.

That victory was important to Foster's later career for it marked him as a "real comer" in the Philadelphia schools. And because of the strong pressures from urban black communities, he also believed that the school system needed him. The constituency which he developed among the "Gratzonians" and the resulting good reputation in the wider black community became important political resources. For it was Foster's ability to utilize his broad environmental support which aided his rapid professional rise; from high school principal in Philadelphia to superintendent of schools in Oakland in a four-year period (1966-1970).

The style of leadership employed by Foster was a "natural" outgrowth of his professional socialization once he became a school principal. School administrators are expected to develop good relations with their communities because they provide them with support to run their schools and because of the widespread belief in community participation in public education. Foster pointedly reminded Oakland's principals of this potential when they began to grumble about his new principal selection process.[4] To Foster, the new process represented an opportunity for Oakland's principals to do something new. Community participation in principal selection would, Foster believed, allow the school administrators to follow the practice he had adopted in building community and staff support at Gratz. The superintendent admitted that school grade levels might pose some problems for the principals. He expected it to be easier to support the leader of an elementary school: "There you are the father figure. . . . It was, 'Mr. Foster, you tell us and we'll do it.' They would bring me their troubles."[5] But as Foster moved to secondary schools, this task required more effort. With some wry humor he spoke of his problems when he became principal at Gratz:

high school . . . teachers are creatures who live on a kind of ambrosia other mortals couldn't exist on. If you don't come through the classic promotion route—high school teacher to department head to vice-principal to principal—you are regarded as some sort of monstrosity. And to come from an elementary school . . . ! On top of this . . . the faculty was openly grumbling because they felt it was wrong to appoint a person "just because he's colored."[6]

In common with other political executives, however, Superintendent Foster sometimes forgot that his talents and skills could not be readily transferred to others. His ability to organize a community and secure staff support did not mean that the Oakland school administrators could do the same. Yet solving Oakland's problems of urban education could not be held in abeyance while his principals were taught the "Foster method" of leadership. Their learning would have to come from watching his performance. Marcus Foster was in a hurry. Oakland's new superintendent saw himself as a practitioner, not a theoretician. It should come as no surprise, therefore, that he believed the innovations which he planned to introduce were "doable." This pragmatic emphasis is consistent with the view which sees politics as "the art of the possible." Foster believed that his innovations were feasible without an extensive investigation of the environment in which they were to operate.

4. See below, p. 53.
5. Foster, *Making Schools Work*, p. 105.
6. Ibid., pp. 105-6.

"COOLING OUT" THE BLACK CAUCUS

For the new superintendent public dissent and political demand-making were symptoms of problems, but they were not the problems themselves. A turbulent political environment reflected a lack of organizational purpose and leadership. While Foster recognized the need to grapple with the highly visible symptoms, he also saw an opportunity, an opening to be seized and converted into a more stable resource of his leadership. It was for such reasons that two of his goals for change in Oakland were designed to improve relations between his organization and its public. If this purpose could be met, there was a likely instrumental value to be achieved as well. Foster believed that better rapport with the community would give him the room to initiate substantial organizational changes. Still, there was the problem of an unsettled political environment in Oakland which Foster had to resolve before much else could be attempted. Any efforts to launch innovations in the public schools, especially those which would span accepted organization boundaries, would be more difficult if the superintendent couldn't stabilize his environment.

As I noted earlier, organized dissent and protest had waned before Foster accepted Oakland's offer. The Black Caucus could no longer mobilize large groups, but it was still viewed as a problem with a potential to reopen old wounds. The organization retained enough influence in Oakland's black community to pose a possible obstacle to the new superintendent. In order to move toward improved relations between the Oakland schools and the black community, Foster would have to find a way to reduce caucus influence in school matters while simultaneously creating his own political base. And these tasks were complicated by Superintendent Foster's need to avoid making enemies early in his term of office. The superintendent chose a single strategy which would, he hoped, give him the information he needed to reduce the risks of the latter while helping him to demonstrate a new climate of relationships.

As far as the caucus was concerned, Foster took office under a cloud. Members of the organization were unhappy that he had refused to meet with them before accepting the superintendency. And they were especially incensed over the coup de grâce by the board president in getting the new superintendent to sign his contract at the airport instead of during the formal ceremonies.

As a result of his doing so, the caucus lost its chance to exploit the publicity which would have attended the normal ceremony in the board room. Outmaneuvered on that front, the Black Caucus tried, unsuccessfully, to place the yoke of being the Board of Education's "handpicked" superintendent on Foster's neck.

These kinds of attacks can be ignored, at the risk of inviting more of the same. Or the person attacked may elect to respond directly with countercharges of his own. Such a response is likely to increase the conflict, however, by exposing the leader to attacks from other quarters which have latent grievances that have previously lain dormant. A third possibility for a leader is to utilize surrogates—men known to be associated with him—to engage his critics.[7] In such instances, the leader frequently assumes the position of an uninvolved third party. From such a vantage point the leader can portray himself as above parochial political conflict. Rather, his concerns for conscientiously carrying out the responsibilities of his office can then be offered as the reason for his refusal to be involved in such matters. Finally, the leader may try to make the accusations work to his own advantage. Although incumbents may employ this approach, it seems especially appropriate to new leaders, because they are usually unencumbered by the organization's past. Early in his tenure Superintendent Foster spoke of new goals and objectives for the Oakland public schools almost as though the school system had no prior experience with goal development. He had already decided that his innovations were technically feasible. And, with the self-confidence based on earlier, though not directly related, successes, Foster believed the changes he wanted were also politically feasible.

BELIEFS INTO PRACTICES

"Political feasibility," Ralph Huitt wrote, ". . . is a term of art. It is a seat-of-the-pants judgment, based on the experiences of the person making it."[8] Community involvement in the selection of Oakland's principals was not based on the experience of other school systems with this practice, but it was based on Foster's

7. This third approach is quite common in political campaigns. It is thought to describe the tactics of President Nixon against Senator McGovern in the 1972 presidential race.

8. Ralph K. Huitt, "Political Feasibility," in *Political Science and Public Policy*, ed. Austin Ranney (Chicago: Rand McNally, 1968), p. 266.

long experience as a black schoolman who had listened to what "representatives of interest groups have said, probably in all honesty, but from a remoteness from the currents that run in the country which only a man who spends [twenty-three years in public education] can have."[9]

Gratz, under Foster's leadership, became a "community-centered school." Such a school, in the words of Preston Wilcox, one of the activists in New York City's I.S. 201 controversy, "functions as an acculturation tool, an educational instrument, and a community center."[10] Foster's opportunity to satisfy these criteria actually came about as the result of another decision made by Philadelphia's central administration. His high school was chosen to "lead the way" in designing ethnically relevant curricula for black secondary students. However, he quickly saw this as a possible means to another goal: "involve students and parents in the process of determining what should be taught."[11] To enhance the concept of *community-centeredness* Foster also initiated services in his school which might customarily be found elsewhere in the city. For example, a "Center for Personal Adjustment" was developed for specialized counseling needs, complemented by a "Youth Opportunity Center" which would acquaint inner-city youths with the world of work. And there were other examples, such as the storefront school which was started in an effort to increase the level of student and parent participation in the schools' activities.[12] These various activities and the successes they achieved convinced Superintendent Foster that community involvement (or shared power) was essential to providing a better education for black youths. Of particular relevance to what Foster envisioned for the Oakland public schools were Wilcox' comments on the redistribution of power through the development of community-centered schools:

The community-centered school . . . deliberately shares power with the community it serves. . . . As a case in point, the community might have the ultimate decision in selecting the principal.[13]

9. Ibid.

10. Preston Wilcox, "The Community-Centered School," in *The Schoolhouse in the City*, ed. Alvin Toffler (New York: Praeger, 1968), p. 100.

11. Foster, *Making Schools Work*, p. 119.

12. Ibid., pp. 121-27.

13. Wilcox, "The Community-Centered School," p. 103.

Superintendent Foster spoke persuasively and often about sharing power, but not simply between a school and its clientele public. Now he spoke of sharing organizational power with the entire community. The similarity between Wilcox' and Foster's ideas was not accidental: the two men had frequent contacts as consultants on black educational issues. In no case, however, did Foster consider giving the power of "ultimate decision" to the community.

Oakland received its first tangible evidence of change within six weeks of Foster's arrival. In August 1970 the superintendent announced the implementation of a new principal selection process.[14] Under this new system applicants for a principal vacancy would be screened and interviewed by a panel of community members and students. The superintendent believed, as did some members of the community, that this process would enable the panel members to "discern such intangible factors as psychological stance, personal qualities, and commitment to uphold local community interests."[15] Despite Foster's rejection of the concept of community control, he was a strong believer in the presumed efficacy of "community input."[16] During his first address to the staff, after the new procedure had been used several times, he offered the following rationale for the plan:

14. For a detailed examination of this process see Jesse J. McCorry, "A Policy Analysis of Resource Allocation in the Oakland Public Schools," unpublished, 1971, chapter 3.

15. Wilcox, "The Community-Centered Schools," p. 103.

16. Leonard J. Fein, *The Ecology of the Public Schools* (New York: Pegasus, 1971), chapters 2-3, gives a sympathetic presentation of the community control concept. He maintains that "Movement towards the assertion of community by blacks is less a sign of failure of the system than a sign of weakness in the theory [of community]. . . . Community control as a social theory is, then, not so much a revolutionary departure as it is the latest chapter in a debate that has gone on for many years" (p. 57). Another favorable assessment of control by blacks of their communities is offered in Alan A. Altshuler, *Community Control: The Black Demand for Participation in Large American Cities* (New York: Pegasus, 1970). Altshuler is particularly useful for his discussion of the issues involved in community control. In his view the issues of black participation center on three values: "political authority, group representation in public bureaucracies and the private income . . . generated by governmental activity" (p. 64). See too the discussion in Stokely Carmichael and Charles Hamilton, *Black Power: The Politics of Liberation in America* (New York: Vintage Books, 1967). Although Carmichael and Hamilton do not specifically consider "community control," their work is often regarded as the ideological rationale for its demand. Also see Milton Kotler, *Neighborhood Government: The Local Foundations of Political Life* (Indianapolis: Bobbs-Merrill, 1969).

a community that has helped to place a principal in his job is committed by that very act to helping the principal succeed. I used to say to
some of my principal friends back East that they didn't have to worry so
much about establishing a union to protect their jobs and their working
conditions. The best kind of job insurance any principal can have is a
faculty, student body, and community at his back saying, "You're doing
the job, brother, keep on."[17]

The slight defensiveness in these remarks reflected an awareness that the new procedure had encountered some opposition.
The school principals stood to lose some influence under this
arrangement.

THE SUBVERSION OF A
SUBORDINATE'S CONSTITUENCY

The leader of an organization may create unanticipated problems for himself as he goes about building his constituency. To
be sure, his efforts to secure supporters are deliberate, but he may
possibly through unrelated practices wean away constituents
from his subordinates.[18] The leader of an organization has the
problem, then, of attempting to secure his own power while
seeming to respect that of others in his organization.

The initiation of lay participation in principal selection illustrates the form which this problem assumed in Oakland. Prior to
the arrival of Dr. Foster, principal selection was handled exclusively by the superintendent's cabinet. Usually one of the
assistant superintendents would choose the individual, and the
other members of the cabinet would ratify the choice, with the
superintendent making the nomination to the board. The board
would then formally announce the appointment.

The introduction of community involvement in the selection
of principals brought a warm response from the community and
the board. It was also a significant step in the development of
Foster's constituency, for it indicated an early awareness and
responsiveness to community demands for participation.

The superintendent did not deliberately set out to erode the
constituency support of the principals in Oakland. He was seeking to make operational his notion of "shared power" between

17. Foster, *Making Schools Work*, p. 157.
18. See the useful discussion of this and related issues in Eugene Litwak,
"Models of Bureaucracy Which Permit Conflict," *American Journal of Sociology* 17 (September 1961): 177-84.

the schools and their public. Nor was Foster aware that his actions in establishing these lay groups undercut a victory only recently won by Oakland's principals. The principals had felt themselves excluded from promotional opportunities by existing principal selection practices. They seldom had a chance to apply for vacancies in higher-ranked schools in the district. The old practice was changed in 1968. Now, only two years later, the principals thought they were again being denied the chance to compete for vacancies. This was not quite true. The new procedures for selection allowed the lay group to establish some of the screening criteria. Since the professional criteria were already established, the lay groups' criteria were largely subjective and affective. The Oakland Principals Association believed that such criteria unfairly discriminated against some of their members, as well as against other district employees who thought they were in line for promotions based upon their service and placement on the "administrative preferred list." Community involvement thus led to some grumbling among the school system's principals, and even one member of Foster's cabinet complained that the public was receiving "most favored" treatment. The superintendent admitted that

the [community selection] process taints its stars and it strips them in the system way, [it] saps energy and enthusiasm. The failure of a principal under the community selection process is regarded as an utter failure. Word gets around fast and a failure is not wanted anywhere.

The impact of a failure to pass the community's screening successfully was especially painful for applicants who came from Oakland's own ranks. There was no longer the cloak of anonymity which may previously have shielded an unsuccessful applicant if he applied for another vacancy. But for the sake of his commitment to community involvement, Foster accepted this risk. He told the cabinet, "their [community] collective judgment may be sounder than our professional judgment. The longer we go with the process, the more they're going to want and that's good!" Nevertheless, Foster knew that he could not afford to have a group of angry principals. The school principals were too important to the success of his other innovations. Anticipating the potential adverse effects of these grievances, Foster reverted to making some principal appointments directly without resorting to community involvement. This led, in its turn, to some criticisms from community members who charged that the superintendent had broken confidence with them. He was able to soften their criticisms, however, through personal meetings with the parent groups. Much of his reasoning in these sessions was based upon his ability to persuade the parents that he was acting for the "good of the district." He also pointed out to them that he needed to have this flexibility if he was to be effective in his job as superintendent. Such arguments, supported by the good will which he had built up through his other initiatives in community participation, persuaded the parents to relent and not press the issue.

Even when Foster made the selection, however, he sought to make appointments which were consistent with what he believed the community selection process might have produced. The exercise of this prerogative had to be used in a way that would not threaten his executive constituency or his organization's survival. As Simon et al. wrote,

If an agency cannot or will not mollify an important group by selecting . . . the group's representatives for key positions, it *can* build up those characteristics of its personnel that appeal to such groups.[19]

Thus Foster would privately seek a community's views on the kind of qualifications they wanted in a new principal. These opinions would then be used by the superintendent as he considered the candidates for a given post. By sharing some of his appointive power with the community, the new superintendent was beginning to create a supportive constituency for his other goals. Any public agency may find it necessary to yield control over a segment of its program to a significant interest group in order to buy the support of that group for more important policy goals. Then, as Rourke observes,

goal distortion of a serious kind is thus always a possible price of constituency support. . . . [G]enerally speaking, in the case of clientele, regulatory, and other administrative agencies, the tendency for capture by an outside group . . . is the greatest when an agency deals with a single-interest constituency.[20]

19. Herbert A. Simon, Donald W. Smithburg, and Victor A. Thompson, *Public Administration* (New York: Alfred A. Knopf, 1950), pp. 414-16; passage cited is found at p. 414, emphasis in original.

20. Francis E. Rourke, *Bureaucracy, Politics, and Public Policy* (Boston: Little, Brown, 1969), pp. 22-23.

School systems' clientele had previously been an example of a single-interest constituency. But with the development of the wide range of special programs, services and activities in public education during the 1960s, this was frequently not the case.

Diverse programs and activities also render demand-making more diffuse because they tend to wean away some dissenters whose interests are being met by one or more of these activities. Diversity in organizational services is also likely to further the development of a broader and more durable base of political support. In turn these developments can lessen the organization's (and the leader's) dependence upon any specific part of the general constituency. It should also be noted that a diversity of activities enhances the ability of the executive to speak authoritatively for his organization, its constituents and clientele. For it is the political executive who is in the best position to draw the discrete activities together into a coherent policy framework. A carefully integrated and thought-out set of programs is an asset to any political executive. Its possession, augmented by skill in its presentation, was part of the way in which Superintendent Foster sought to gain support among Oakland's significant political actors.

"TOUCHING BASE" WITH THE "POWER ELITE"

Although most of Superintendent Foster's efforts to build a political base were directed to the mass public, he did not neglect the "influentials" in the city. Just as he needed "scouts" to gain access to some minority communities in Oakland, so too he found that his board members were willing to do the same with the local business and commercial influentials. While still in Philadelphia, Foster and his deputy Blackburn decided to "touch base with the politicos" because of Oakland's financial problems, and a board member arranged meetings with Oakland's delegation in the California legislature and through them with the governor.

Despite the board protestations that they had no particular constituencies, Foster quickly discerned a liberal to moderate conservative division. Thus, the one Democrat on the board introduced him to labor leaders and the liberal element in the community. And the high-ranking corporate officer on the board did the same with leaders of Oakland's business and commercial community.

The labor organizations would have an interest in what Foster would attempt to do in Oakland. The school system's labor force consisted of a large number of union members, especially in the building and craft trades. Union leaders would naturally be interested in anything happening in the school system which might affect the traditional "bread and butter" concerns of their membership.

With the economic influentials, however, Foster's inducements to gain their support were less tangible even than they were for his lay public. He could stress a common interest in the need for more efficiency and he could talk about his intention to involve the private sector in providing work experiences for the students. But generally Foster tried to play on the sense of social responsibility which had begun to emerge in the business community in response to the "urban crisis." The one specific but unspoken benefit which they could expect in return was a community with little or no racial conflict in its schools with Foster as superintendent.

Initially these occasions were not used for substantive conversations about the proposed changes in the schools. After all, the board had not yet seen Foster's detailed plans. But these meetings did give the superintendent an opportunity to "sketch" his educational philosophy. In addition, these informal discussions gave further evidence of Foster's determination to make the schools a part of the total community, and left the door ajar for later discussions.

CONSTITUENCY-BUILDING IN MULTI-RACIAL COMMUNITIES

As a black political executive, Superintendent Foster's race gave him some advantages in dealing with non-white citizens in Oakland. Despite the popularized belief in "third world solidarity," however, Foster's minority status did not provide him with automatic access to all non-white associations and groups. The superintendent needed "guides" who could help him find his way in the Native American and Asian-American communities. As urban bureaucracies enlarged their non-white staffs the ability to gain such access through organizational members was enhanced. Fortunately for Dr. Foster's plans, the schools had some staff members who could help arrange meetings with representatives of the minority communities in Oakland.

Some of these communities, such as the Filipinos and Native Americans, were small and poorly organized. That is, they lacked a record of public participation which would have made their spokespersons known to the wider community and thus easier to approach. Here the superintendent had a resource that may not be available to other urban political executives. It was a relatively simple matter to use the children from these communities to act as messengers to their parents. Foster had no grand expectations regarding the outcome of this effort, but it was his responsibility to take the initiative in developing a working relationship. Such efforts might pay off by demonstrating his own good intentions and accessibility as the head of the schools. The superintendent believed that this would be an adequate basis upon which to establish a degree of community trust.

WHO SPEAKS FOR WHAT GROUP?

The multi-racial character of Oakland's population and the diversity of voluntary associations imposed an added burden on Foster's efforts. It was difficult to know who was representative of what. This was especially true among the Chinese-speaking organizations and for the Spanish-speaking community. A man from Philadelphia, where such problems were "black and white," could be forgiven his ignorance. In the Chinese community Foster's problem stemmed from a split between newly arrived immigrant students from Hong Kong, who had particular educational needs based on inadequate English speaking and reading ability plus genuine culture shock, and those Chinese-speaking students who came from established families in the city. The latter group was also concerned about culture, but from the ideological perspective of the "third world." This difficulty was further complicated by alleged delinquency and criminal activities by the immigrant youths against the resident youths while in school. In the Spanish-speaking community, the new superintendent was confronted by several groups, each of which Foster thought was represented in the city-wide Spanish-speaking Unity Council. Again, however, there were intragroup conflicts which the new superintendent did not initially recognize, but to which he was expected to respond. Foster chose the simplifying strategy of treating no single group as *the* representative of the diverse interests in these ethnic and racial communities. Instead he adopted the practice he had followed in dealing with the Black Caucus. That is, each group which claimed their community's imprimatur was treated as a representative of a legitimate point of view which entitled the group to be heard. Of course, the superintendent's solution did little to stimulate greater unity among these competing groups. But his decision, and its acceptance by the various groups, made it possible for Foster to proceed with his efforts to develop broad community support in spite of the divisions.

The success of a simplifying strategy for becoming acquainted with his constituency rested upon the superintendent's ability to keep its various components in a state of "dynamic equilibrium." He suggested that some of his colleagues in the East had made the mistake of spending too much time with one group, and because these political executives gave so much of their time to militant blacks they failed to hear what either the black or white middle classes were saying. Foster believed the black middle class to be especially important because it wanted the same services as the militants. The only difference between the two, in his view, was that the militants wanted them faster. And we must remember that most of the key members in the Black Caucus were, at least in income terms, middle class.

Regardless of Foster's initiation of community involvement in principal selection and his strides in developing effective communications with his diverse public, he realized that his base was fragile. Nonetheless, these first efforts bought him some time in which to maneuver. The superintendent had made a specific response to a salient community interest, and his willingness to listen was enough to moderate some demands which could not be met immediately. Although these were substantive matters, they were also part of Foster's style.

Some critics argue that style does little but connote disingenuousness. Murray Edelman, for example, maintains that "leaders rely increasingly on style differences to create and emphasize an impression of maneuverability, and the impression remains an important political fact even if the maneuverability is not."[21] However, one can raise a more fundamental objection to Edel-

---

21. Murray Edelman, *The Symbolic Uses of Politics* (Champaign, Illinois: University of Illinois Press, 1967), p. 74; see also Erving Goffman, *The Presentation of Self in Everyday Life* (New York: Anchor Books, 1959), chapter 6.

man's view. Virtually all positions of public leadership contain institutionalized characteristics even if they are only symbolic. This is not the same as saying that these features are trivial and unimportant. If they had been trivial, the charge of failing to set a proper moral tone for the country would not have weighed so heavily with the general public in regard to President Nixon's troubles with Watergate. Nor should we deprecate the symbolic value of the president as the representative of the nation on state occasions.

In a similar way the personalities and styles of urban political executives are inevitably associated with their tenure in office. And if the impact is sufficiently strong (for whatever reason) their tenure is typed and some of their idiosyncratic features may become part of the permanent appurtenances of the office in question. Thus it is common to hear people refer to "Mayor Daley's Chicago" or "Mayor Lindsay's New York." The way all of his duties are performed, especially the ritualistic and symbolic, becomes a cue for the public in making judgments about a leader's incumbency. Some political systems may in fact be so structured that little remains of a political executive's role save its symbolism. Such, for example, may be the case in a city which has a mayor and strong city manager, as in Oakland, where the mayor has little more than ritualistic duties to perform. And despite his executive title, the mayor in such a system is frequently regarded (and acts) as just another council member on questions of policy.

Foster, however, wanted to do more than create an impression of maneuverability. His insistence on controlling the agenda for change in the schools and his refusal to accept the "donated dignity" offered by the Oakland Black Caucus support the view that he wanted the fact of maneuverability and flexibility to be seen as important components of his leadership. He was intent on exercising the type of leadership in his system that Burns had in mind for presidents:

It is to build new institutions that will be capable of shaping political and other human behavior into patterns legitimized by the ideology of the leadership and of the electorate. . . . The emphasis is on goals rather than methods, on change rather than stability, on context rather than process, on innovation rather than routine, on creativity rather than adaptation. Efficiency, keeping the machine running, the handling of routine problems—these are secondary matters.[22]

22. James MacGregor Burns, *Presidential Government* (Boston: Houghton Mifflin, 1956), p. 195.

Foster, as we saw earlier, had strong beliefs about change in public education and what would be required to make those changes a reality in Oakland. But, as we will see in later chapters, successful implementation of change depends upon effectively handling precisely those matters which Burns dismisses as "routine problems."

Community involvement was one of the changes which Foster wanted to introduce. The superintendent made it clear, however, that what he proposed was not community control. His initial speech to his staff elaborated his belief:

> I have alluded to the importance of community involvement. I am not talking about window dressing. A school insulated from its community never was a good idea. Nowadays, it is impossible. The people must have meaningful roles in making decisions in order for them to have legitimate means of expressing their power. . . .
>
> In this context, we are developing a multiple-option approach to community involvement. This is based on the notion that communities and schools vary in their readiness to enter into strong partnerships. Some will wish to continue the parent-teacher association format. Others may prefer a more formal arrangement, perhaps an advisory board arrangement where community people sit down and hear what the principal has to say and offer advice and suggestions. Finally, there will be those communities ready to say, "let us have a part in the formal decision-making process."
>
> Notice, I keep talking about community participation in the decision-making process. I am not talking about community control because there is no such thing as community control. Schools are state institutions. We are bound by state statutes; many of our powers simply cannot be given to the communities. But we can *share*, in increasingly effective ways, our decision-making prerogatives. While the school site will be the place where such transactions will take place, the central office will be committed to assisting you and making necessary resources available. It will be our responsibility to see that the notion of community involvement stretches beyond the single schools and encompasses the entire city.[23]

This strong position also effectively ended the discussion of community control of the schools in Oakland, which had not been a major issue in any case.

Citizen involvement was also to include the development of a Master Plan Citizens Committee (the MPCC). "This broadly

23. Foster, *Making Schools Work*, pp. 157-88.

representative body," Foster told his listeners, "will devote itself to plans for delivering uniformly excellent school facilities for our students and staff."[24]

Initially, then, the MPCC was given a limited charge by the superintendent. But before the formation of this body was formally announced, Foster, his deputy, and some staff members decided that broad community involvement meant that planning for the physical plant had to be joined with the other aspects of the educational process. Thus the MPCC was made a district-wide body with a number of task forces to examine specific parts of the educational program. By giving the community group this much broader mandate Superintendent Foster hoped they would come to understand the range of problems with which he had to deal. If this understanding developed, he believed, it could lead to more cooperative relations between the schools and the public. In addition, Foster also anticipated that the community's increased knowledge of the conditions of the public schools would reduce the number of conflicting demands for limited organizational resources.

KEEP COMMUNITY PARTICIPATION IN CHECK

In spite of Superintendent Foster's strong belief in the value of community involvement, we have seen that he also believed just as strongly in his own responsibility as the head of the school system. The adoption of community involvement did not imply a "commitment to run everything by the MPCC." That is, prior community approval was not contemplated for all administration decisions. "If they can be brought along with us, fine," he continued, "if not, to hell with them! Community participation shouldn't be a brake on the exercise of [our] best professional judgments in a given issue."

The work of the MPCC task force studying school finances provides another example of how Foster would sometimes limit the actions of the community. The draft report of the MPCC task force in school finance was a disappointment to Foster. He regarded the report as the product of a study group while he wanted an action-oriented document. The report was useless, he believed, "because there are no marching orders"; it couldn't be used to

24. Ibid., p. 158.

point to a next step in solving a critical school problem. Because of these deficiencies the superintendent told the community group and its consultants to reexamine and revise some sections before submission to the Board of Education. After returning the report Foster told his cabinet that it was "good for the administration to hedge, it keeps the task forces from thinking we've *got* to go with their recommendations." These comments reveal some of the frustrations of a political executive who has attempted to share power, while he tries to retain the prerogatives of his office. Foster was able to set these limits on community efforts to acquire more power because they trusted him not to misuse his office.

The consequences of community involvement in Oakland were unknowable, but Foster was convinced that his innovation would work, despite the lack of evidence. The MPCC was Foster's answer to the question of what the most appropriate form for the relations between a public bureaucracy and the public is. And even if he were to be proved wrong, the superintendent might have taken comfort in George Gallup's observation:

> People tend to judge a man by his goals, by what he is trying to do, and not *necessarily* by what he accomplishes or by how well he succeeds. . . . If people are convinced you are trying to meet problems and that you are aware of their problems and are trying to do something about them, they don't hold you responsible for 100 per cent success. Nor do you have to have any great ideas on how to accomplish the ends.[25]

Obviously, the MPCC did not constitute a formal decision-making unit for the school system, but its creation did represent a step toward making the bureaucracy more responsive and accountable.[26] However, leaders who attempt to institute changes, in

25. *Opinion Polls: Interviews by Donald McDonald with Elmo Roper and George Gallup* (Santa Barbara, California, 1962), quoted by Edelman, op. cit., pp. 78-79, emphasis added. Gallup's comments about the public's limited expectations notwithstanding, Foster's insistence upon his own personal accountability for goal achievement made the task of evaluating his performance easier than might ordinarily be the case. He gave the public and members of his organization a "measuring stick." And he was to find that many of those who had heard him or read his statement in September 1970 were not reluctant to put this instrument to use.

26. A comparable effort to improve government responsiveness has been described by the mayor of Boston. See Kevin White, "Boston's Little City Halls," in *Political Power and the Urban Crisis*, 3rd ed., edited by Alan Shank (Boston: Holbrook Press, 1976), pp. 278-86.

either a political system or a public bureaucracy, and who come to symbolize the goals they espouse face another challenge.

Despite the financial autonomy of the MPCC, much of its effectiveness would be based upon the superintendent's support. Similarly, Foster had put his own prestige behind his new creation. Thus, he and the citizens were intimately bound up with the participatory goals which were so strongly expressed.

Superintendent Foster had no difficulty in accepting the personal responsibility, but he was aware of the more general problem. He defined it in terms of a difference between charisma and getting solid accomplishments. "The charismatic leader . . . is good for getting things off the ground," he stated, "but they don't follow through and that's where the problems are."[27] The simple expression of new goals to be achieved was not enough. But the creation of new organizational goals and values was an important first step in change. As Simon, Smithburg and Thompson wrote in commenting on this problem of organizational support:

In general, the inducements to external supporters come from the goals and objectives of governmental organizations or the values created by them. Even as the customer of a commercial organization is interested in its produce, so the "customers" of governmental organizations are interested in the products of governmental action. They give their support, their contribution to the organization, in return for the satisfactions they derive from the values created by the organization, whether these be increased educational opportunity or national defense.[28]

The rewards which Foster promised to his constituency could only come at some future time, that is, when the goals were achieved. In this regard we can treat the adoption of the two modes of community participation as short-range goals.

In his discussion of the "instrumental functions of leadership" Downton states:

27. The problem alluded to is not unique to the Oakland case. A poignant example is found in the fate of Prince Sihanouk's regime in Cambodia shortly after Buchanan wrote: "The extent to which he [Sihanouk] can continue to maintain the political cohesion of the Community—and the stability of Cambodia—depends very largely on his personal contact with the masses and on his personal prestige which is intimately bound up with the [policies] . . . he so passionately expounds." Keith Buchanan, "Cambodian Royal Socialism," in *Leadership and Authority: A Symposium,* ed. Gehan Wijeyewardene (Singapore: University of Malaya Press, 1968), sponsored by UNESCO, p. 261.

28. Herbert A. Simon, Donald W. Smithburg and Victor A. Thompson, *Public Administration* (New York: Alfred A. Knopf, 1950), p. 386.

leadership must make adjustments in two essentially distinct goal hierarchies. Preferences must be selected among a number of *general* goals, which are the distant objectives of the . . . system. Then more immediate and short-range goals have to be ordered as a means of reaching the generalized ends. These short-range goals make up the *particular* goal hierarchy.[29]

The general goals which the superintendent set for schools, efficiency in resource allocations and improved student performance, had an impact on the *particular* goal hierarchy. An effective participative role for the community was the keystone of that hierarchy.

In setting his goals for the organization, establishing effective forms of communications, and actively persuading others to accept those goals, Foster's instrumental leadership became the base upon which "a positive transactional commitment" could be made by his constituency.[30]

Since the followers' rewards for entering the transaction are expected rather than immediate, Downton states "it is especially important that communication networks be well-developed, for a leader-follower pattern formed through positive transactions is contingent on the leader's knowledge of followers' demands and needs."[31]

While Downton is specifically interested in "rebel" as opposed to "ruling" leadership we can see that Foster, a ruling leader in Downton's scheme, was more than willing to adapt those features of a rebel leadership style to meet the environmental circumstances of his organization.

POLITICAL ACTION WITH CONSTITUENTS

Although public education will continue to require political executives with good management skills, they will also have to add a new dimension to this capability. The public schools, like many urban bureaucracies, have a growing need for leaders with political sensitivity and skill to balance the demands of a fragmented and sometimes volatile constituency within the limits of

29. James V. Downton, Jr., *Rebel Leadership: Commitment and Charisma in the Revolutionary Process* (New York: The Free Press, 1973), pp. 26-29; the passage cited is at p. 26.

30. Downton gives an insightful interpretation of the commitment process in *Rebel Leadership*, chapter 3.

31. Ibid., p. 75.

their organizations' capacities. And the political requirement will apply especially in those areas where the public schools are independent of the city's governmental structure. For, in a city like Oakland, the schools

have no network of support from groups and interests for whom the educators have done favors in the past and who now can be asked to reciprocate. They may sometimes get teachers and the parents and the children to ring doorbells, but such efforts are often ineffectual compared to the canvassing a strong party organization might do.[32]

Foster recognized very early that some of the problems he faced in running the school district could not be solved through his efforts alone. Help would have to be found outside the boundaries of his organization.

Oakland had no strong party organization to which the superintendent could turn and any effort to introduce open partisanship into the city's politics would have met strong resistance from city leaders and the general public. Lacking traditional political resources, the superintendent sought to create his own. One such resource was the MPCC, which Foster mobilized to bring pressure upon the City Council when he asked the city to levy a tax increase to help erase a deficit in the 1971 school budget.

When the superintendent appeared before the council with this request, he brought along a group of supporters drawn from the MPCC. Because there is little overt partisanship in the city's public affairs, this group covered the political spectrum, and because council members and members of the Board of Education drew support from the same electoral base (all elections are at large) Foster reasoned that the implications for potential voter opposition if the council didn't levy the tax were clear. His strategy was to make the City Council appear to be the last source of financial assistance and the only agency that could prevent the teachers' organizations from carrying out a strike threat if they were denied raises.

In making this proposal, the superintendent cast the council into the uncomfortable role of a court of last resort. He indicated that no other revenue source looked promising. Some of the council members, however, were afraid that this would be the start of an annual pattern. One councilman caustically com-

32. Robert H. Salisbury, "School and Politics in the Big City," *Harvard Educational Review* 37 (Summer 1967): 416.

mented: "Is there light at the end of the tunnel . . . what will happen next year? Is there any reason to believe that you will not be back again asking for the same twenty-five cents?" Fortunately, no one raised the obvious example from Foster's past: the Philadelphia schools had depended on the city for several years. The mayor pointed out that the voters had turned the schools down again and again on tax overrides. "Now you are asking another taxing authority to supplement your funds to the contrary of voter sentiment." Here we find one of the interesting dilemmas of politics in nonpartisan cities: the superintendent's supporters in the council chambers represented those who would be most likely to vote for a tax increase in a general election. The councilmen, however, were responding to a different public—the one which had consistently voted against school tax increases since 1958. The superintendent's first effort to use the MPCC for political support had failed. Or had it?

The school system was obviously in trouble. Thus Foster was persuaded by his board to return to the council with a smaller request which would restore positions but provide no salary increases. This was a sore point because of President Nixon's imposition of a wage-price freeze. Although the reductions were made in areas of the budget which were covered by special override taxes (that is, taxes which the board could impose without voter approval) they affected areas with high public impact: preschool, handicapped student programs, instruction for the mentally retarded, and meals for needy children. These cuts were certain to attract attention to the superintendent's efforts. Nevertheless this smaller request was also turned down. Following this defeat, the superintendent issued a press release in which the blame was squarely placed on the City Council:

Speaking on behalf of thousands of Oakland parents, students and concerned citizens, I must express my bitter disappointment that the City Council has refused to support our modest request for financial assistance. Operating under a general tax rate set in 1958, the schools are finally faced with the ugly reality of reducing, rather than improving, services to children.

The facts concerning the schools' plight are well-known to leaders and laymen alike, both in Oakland and Sacramento. We have worked through our elected officials in Washington to secure more federal aid for our district. Five hundred parents and citizens journeyed to the legislature, to testify in support of state aid, which has declined in the last 15 years from nearly 50% to 25% of Oakland's school budget. With no action forthcoming from Sacramento, either from the legislature or the Governor's office, we had no choice but to seek temporary relief from our own City Council.

The results from Council's refusal to act are sad to contemplate. We must now set about to curtail our staff and programs in those ways which will cause the least harm to our schoolchildren. We have slightly more than $200,000 to use to meet a need of several million dollars. I can only hope that the board and our employee groups will find a way to come to those agreements which will make possible the orderly opening of school in September.[33]

It should also be noted that Foster spoke on behalf of a community interest in response to the council's action and not as the spokesman for the school system. To secure his relations with his constituency he seemed to believe it was necessary to divorce himself from his organizational position and his own involvement in the plight of the school system.

The school district finally got almost exactly what it had requested in the reduced proposal. However, these funds came from an award of Emergency Employment Act funds and not local taxes. The council was given very little credit for sharing these monies with the schools. The superintendent, on the other hand, was regarded as having pressed the community's interests so skillfully that the council couldn't refuse to give him a part of these funds. Although the executive constituency had only limited involvement in the outcome they saw themselves as having contributed to it. Thus they could share a sense of having been powerful.

A POLITICAL BASE
MUST NOT LOOK LIKE POLITICS

In Oakland one gets the impression that politics is a dirty word. There is little one can immediately identify as urban political activity. Party affiliations or references are seldom mentioned except for national or state-wide elections. The nonpartisan, good-government tradition of municipal administration is alive and flourishing. Foster's political environment contained only a weak sense of partisan allegiance.

This sparsely populated political environment provides excel-

33. Oakland Public Schools, Office of Public Information, Press Release, "City Council Refuses Financial Assistance to Oakland Schools," 12 August 1971. (Mimeographed.)

lent opportunities for a leader who is sensitive to his personal and organizational resource needs. For example, in a recent school bond election which was being held at the same time as elections for the City Council, the Democratic party organization informally passed out its slate of endorsements through a "get out the vote" effort in support of the school measure. At the same time, however, this kind of environment also signals the existence of a constraint on political activity. The low level of public political activity is not simply a temporary phenomenon in Oakland; it is part of the political culture of the city. This seems to be especially the case when one speaks about the purposes and objectives of public organizations or city government as a whole. Oakland's residents expect their public organizations to serve the commonweal. Any obstacle to that end—and politics is viewed as just such an obstacle—is to be avoided.

For the professional administrator, to be seen as a political actor is somehow regarded as unprofessional conduct. It is not difficult to imagine, then, what might ensue if the public decided that its educational leader were "political." The public unfortunately tends to see the public school system as removed from politics. After all, one of the reasons why many school systems are independent of their formal city governments lies in the desire to remove the schools from the hurly-burly of the political marketplace. In so doing, however, the public has weakened the ability of organizational leaders to be a "double first," in the words of Harlan Cleveland. He explained by noting that the public "instinctively demands that our Presidents be . . . great politicians and great administrators too."[34] Citizens of reform cities such as Oakland appear to believe that by decreeing nonpartisanship in elections and independence for the school system, a superintendent may ignore the political requirement. But the two are inseparable, for none of the political executive's decisions are *purely administrative*, or purely anything else. As Superintendent Foster observed in talking about the political aspects of his job:

When you're dealing with a 90 million dollar budget looking for alternative uses of funds, it's not enough to be seen as the good guy—that doesn't buy you any credit!

34. Harlan Cleveland, "The Executive and the Public Interest," *The Annals of the American Academy of Political and Social Science* 307 (September 1956): 37.

When the Board of Education signed Marcus Foster to a four-year contract they had only resolved one part, albeit a critical part, ot their search for new leadership. They knew the kinds of ideas their new superintendent would bring with him. But they did not know the precise form those ideas would take. Community involvement was something they wanted, but the Board of Education could not be expected to look on this procedure in Foster's terms. For the board, community involvement meant that public dissent was lessened. To the new superintendent, however, this change was a means to augment his political resources. The constituency developed through shared power was to be an instrument of his leadership. Meeting the administrative part of the "instinctive demands" involves less publicly visible actions. Still, the executive must find support. For this task, however, he looks within the organization to fashion a "leadership core," the infrastructure of bureaucratic leadership.

For a political executive who is concerned with innovation and new organizational directions these are critical choices, because much of his reputation is based upon the performance of many others. Constituency and board support are valuable because they contribute to the development of a permissive or restrictive organizational environment. But another critical determinant of what an organization can and will do is based on the individuals whom a leader selects to fill key positions. In the following chapter we look at Foster's men, his "leadership core."

4

Selecting the Superintendent's Men

With the exception of the new principal selection process, Marcus Foster's first months in office produced little change in the administration of the schools. Popular expectations of major staff changes or reorganization went unfulfilled. The new superintendent did not want to "send shock waves" through the organization.

In part, Superintendent Foster's delay in making changes within his organization reflected his awareness that such moves were likely to encounter resistance. While some bureaucratic resistance to change is inevitable, it need not be based upon hostility to a new political executive. Indeed the resistance to change may simply be indicative of a more subtle phenomenon, as Richard Carlson suggested:

At a time of change loyalty enhances the possibility that the following crucial organizational needs will be satisfied—(a) stability of lines of authority and communication, (b) stability of informal relations within the organization, and (c) homogeneity of outlook with respect to the meaning and role of the organization.[1]

And just as Superintendent Foster took time to assess the permissiveness of his external environment for change, his cir-

1. Richard O. Carlson, *Executive Succession and Organizational Change* (Chicago: Midwest Administration Center, University of Chicago, 1962), p. 45.

cumspection with the internal environment served a similar purpose. He knew that his succession and his plans for innovation
would inevitably, as Bernard Levenson has observed, set in motion "a chain reaction in the organization. . . . Succession does
not involve a single personnel transaction but rather a chain of
transactions."[2]

Nevertheless, Foster realized that as an outsider his success
would be defined in terms of the changes he had promised at the
time of his appointment. His commitment to change "coupled
with a lack of ready-made support [made] it clear . . . that he [had]
reason to 'retool' the organization."[3] At the very least the new
superintendent would have to develop what Sarason calls

a core group . . . usually a handful of people who will be closest to [him]
interpersonally and statuswise. They will be "his family" to whom he
delegates responsibilities and powers second only to his own; [the
leader] is quite aware that if he chooses badly he jeopardizes [his]
future.[4]

To make these choices wisely requires time and knowledge; consequently a political executive is unlikely to make these decisions
early. Moreover, just as the executive is "feeling his way," the
members of the organization likewise adopt a "wait and see"
posture.

Yet the organization is doing more than simply marking time;
it continues to carry out routines, even as it watches the new man
settle in. The new leader has greater flexibility and choice during
this period before he becomes accustomed to his new environment. But flexibility and choice under such circumstances may
also increase the potential for error. Foster approached this critical task of leadership conservatively.

THE INHERITED "LEADERSHIP CORE"

Foster could have moved quickly to select a new cabinet. His
discretion to act was enhanced because he was new and because
personnel changes were expected by organizational members and

2. Bernard Levenson, "Bureaucratic Succession," in *Complex Organizations: A Sociological Reader*, ed. Amitai Etzioni (New York: Holt, Rinehart and
Winston, 1961), p. 363.

3. Carlson, *Executive Succession*, p. 45.

4. Seymour B. Sarason, *The Creation of Settings and the Future Societies*
(San Francisco: Jossey-Bass, 1972), p. 73.

the general constituency. But the new superintendent's early behavior gave little indication of his intentions. Rather, Foster delayed in selecting his leadership core in order to show his new staff that the new political executive was "coming to terms with the organization."[5] And there was more involved as well. Foster was engaged in a serious "effort not only to reshape the alignment of group interests behind [the] administration, but to reshape the institutional framework within which the political leader seeks to realize his goals."[6] The latter of these purposes was pursued indirectly through the weekly cabinet meetings. By continuing these meetings Foster maintained a tradition which provided him with valuable on-the-job training.

In addition, had the superintendent moved early to change the composition of this leadership group, he might have jeopardized the success of his own goals. By continuing with his inherited cabinet and the routines of the accustomed twice-weekly meetings, Foster economized on the amount of time he had to devote to learning. By listening carefully and asking astute questions, the new superintendent was able to pick the brains of men with extensive knowledge of the Oakland public schools. Foster's own lengthy experience in public education notwithstanding, the specific, local experience of these men was an invaluable resource. He would have been foolish not to make use of their knowledge.

Two members of the inherited cabinet were especially valuable. Dr. Spencer Benbow, the former business manager and Foster's immediate predecessor, had more than forty years' experience in the Oakland schools. His career spanned virtually all levels of the organizational hierarchy. Benbow's value to the new superintendent resulted from his fifteen years of involvement in developing the school district's budget. As a consequence he was a repository of detailed information on financial matters. Moreover, the former business manager possessed equally detailed knowledge of the organization's structure and practices. The second person to whom Foster could turn was the assistant superintendent for elementary instruction, a man with only slightly less experience (thirty years) than the business manager. Although specifically responsible for elementary education, this

5. James McGregor Burns, *Presidential Government* (Boston: Houghton Mifflin, 1965), p. 199.
6. Carlson, *Executive Succession*, p. 24.

assistant superintendent was frequently involved in the secondary instructional program. His colleague in charge of that level was comparatively new to Oakland, and was generally thought to be less knowledgeable and effective in his job. The head of elementary instruction could give Foster considerable insight into the principals because he had trained many of them. His knowledge was enhanced by the tendency of these principals to seek his advice on matters of substance affecting their schools. The assistant superintendent for secondary instruction was valuable because of his detailed understanding of the state's education code.

The newest member of the cabinet, and its only black member, was the assistant superintendent for urban educational services. His value to the new superintendent derived from his close ties in Oakland's black community. In addition, he was responsible for the school district's extensive compensatory education program, which comprised approximately 10 percent of the annual budget. The last of the cabinet members was the director of research. The only specialist among this leadership group, he was also the only one lacking classroom experience. But he was a good facts-and-figures man and could give Foster useful information on the testing and evaluation of students and the impact of various programs in which the schools were involved. In addition, he was the "board representative" in negotiations with teachers' organizations. Thus he could help Foster by keeping him abreast of developments among the teaching staff. And his experience as a negotiator would be useful in giving the new superintendent some insight into the composition of these teacher groups.[7]

The new superintendent made only one change in the cabinet (other than adding his deputy) when he took office: he added the director of personnel, another black administrator, because that had been the practice in the Philadelphia schools and

7. Oakland teachers could join either the Oakland Federation of Teachers (AFT) or the Oakland Education Association (NEA). In particular, the nature of the conflicts between these two groups could perhaps provide the superintendent with an advantage in bargaining, especially since the federation represented less than a quarter of Oakland's certified [professional] personnel and was trying to increase its membership. Foster's concern regarding the teacher organizations was essentially to learn what their tactics might be—that is, would they be likely to call a strike in protest against some decision of the administration.

because doing so furthered Foster's "salt and pepper" rule within this important leadership group. That is, Foster wanted to make certain that the key leadership positions in the organization would be integrated. In this regard, the new superintendent was explicitly race-conscious as he filled senior and middle-management (principal and others) positions. These changes had some symbolic value to the organization's attentive public, but there was still little perceptible difference in the way the organization did things. The move did not represent the kind of change which many observers, inside and outside the organization, believed necessary to correct the faults of the Oakland public schools.

The members of this organizational elite were not entirely unknown to Superintendent Foster. He already knew something about them as a result of their written responses to his requests for analyses of, and recommendations for, the district's educational program. In addition, Price-Waterhouse and Company, the management consultant firm, had provided him with informal senior personnel evaluations. These pieces of intelligence notwithstanding, Foster waited to see the members of his cabinet in their own milieu before making his selections. Moreover, he did not make his judgments solely on the basis of past performance; rather, the superintendent was looking for men who could perform in a redesigned organization and a changed political environment. Foster had in mind the creation of what Richard F. Fenno, Jr., describes as the "ideal Cabinet" of a president:

made up of men who are eminently fitted to perform special tasks, yet [who] must cohere as a unit if the name Cabinet is to have more than honorific significance.[8]

Thus, Foster's salt and pepper rule became a functional equivalent of political "balance" in his choices.[9]

Prior to taking over the job, Superintendent Foster had been told that the cabinet was not particularly well liked by members of the Board of Education. In the past the superintendent's cabinet had been used as a collective decisionmaking body. That is, many of the decisions made by the senior staff members of the

8. Richard F. Fenno, Jr., *The President's Cabinet* (New York: Vintage Books, 1959), p. 64.
9. Ibid., pp. 77-81.

Oakland public schools were announced as cabinet decisions. Board members who were concerned about this procedure were in fact concerned with the style rather than the substance of the decisions in question. They wanted to be able to affix responsibility for a particular decision and also to hold accountable those who had the responsibility for following through on a given decision. In other words, the board wanted the superintendent— *their* chief executive—to say, "*I* have decided" rather than "the cabinet has decided." The board could easily hold the superintendent accountable because his was the total administrative responsibility for the organization. It was no problem for Foster to accept the board's preference. Their view was entirely consistent with his own wish to be regarded as *the* chief executive of the organization.

THE LEADER'S ALLY

Foster may have been unwilling to initiate wide-ranging personnel changes, but he did make one significant personnel decision: he brought his deputy with him from Philadelphia. Oakland's board members were prepared for this because their consultants had recommended that such a position be created. This was prudent advice in view of the fact that the board wanted the new superintendent to devote considerable effort to strengthening the school system's relations with the community. Someone had to be available to run the shop.

Robert Blackburn, the deputy superintendent of schools, had worked with Foster for one year in the Office of Community Relations in Philadelphia prior to coming to Oakland. However, they had come to know each other well and had also worked together on some "guerilla theater"[10] projects for the Philadelphia schools. In choosing Blackburn, Foster knew that he was getting a deputy who shared many, if not all, of his views of the needs of urban education, as well as a willingness to take risks.

Selecting a white deputy was an early key example of what Foster meant by "salt and pepper." But it also was intended to convey a message to some black constituents that the new superintendent trusted Bob Blackburn. He wanted those who feared

10. These projects were a variation on the sensitivity training model which was frequently used in the late sixties as a way to get blacks and whites to communicate.

that a white man would subvert his authority to see that there was no cause to worry. Nevertheless, he and Blackburn were aware of the possibility that some constituents, black and white, might attempt to erode their close relationship.

Blackburn was most concerned about the responses of black constituents to his presence. Thus he was pleased when one of the black board members privately cautioned him about some white efforts to erode the close relationship he enjoyed with Foster. Blackburn treated this comment as an indication that he was not seen as a potential threat to the superintendent by blacks.

When Foster brought his deputy into office with him he also introduced a new position. The new position created some problems of adjustment for members of the organization. As Oscar Grusky experimentally demonstrated:

Succession of an executive with an ally was shown to alter greatly the formal structure of organizational authority. The introduction of a new executive with a personally selected staff member led to the creation of a level of authority not previously existent in the organization.[11]

Succession with an ally also posed some subtle problems for the superintendent's relations with his board. The members of the Board of Education were accustomed to dealing directly with their chief executive officer. And despite their recognition of Foster's need for a deputy, Blackburn's presence was frequently an obstacle to their attempts to gain direct access to the superintendent. Often a board member's call to Foster was directed to Blackburn by the superintendent's secretary if Foster were out of the office or engaged elsewhere in the administration building. Gradually the board members realized that they no longer had exclusive confidential relationships with Superintendent Foster. In part this was a deliberate strategy on Foster's part. He wished to be seen as independent of the board ("familiarity breeds contempt") as well as independent of organized interest groups among his constituents.

It is worth noting at this point that both Foster and Blackburn disliked the traditional hierarchical model of organizations. The deputy superintendent believed that "the classic hierarchical model . . . a formal chain of command, is simply not applicable in

11. Oscar Grusky, "Succession with an Ally," *Administrative Science Quarterly* 14, no. 2 (June 1969): 170.

urban school systems. The task involved in running [school] systems simply do not permit that kind of clean structural arrangement."

It is difficult to know exactly what the relationship between Foster and Blackburn was if you look only at the paper description, because Blackburn drew up his own job description. On matters such as personnel, Blackburn acted with almost complete autonomy. Checking the board meeting agenda and making sure that specific issues raised by board members had been carried out by the responsible parties within the administration was another area in which the deputy acted independently and would simply inform the superintendent. Blackburn also cleared releases from the Public Information Office, research publications, and project reports from the various project offices in the district.

The superintendent and his deputy developed a division of labor which resembled the often cited "inside-outside" syndrome. Blackburn filled the inside role while Foster dealt with the school system's public. Thus the deputy superintendent spent most of his working day in the district's central office. He seldom left the building during the lunch hour, preferring instead to grab a sandwich from the lunchroom's vending machines. The superintendent was seldom merely out to lunch. His lunch hour was just another part of his workday. Much of the deputy's time was spent in handling what he called "minor stuff." This tended to be numerous community relations questions, and since he and Foster had shared experiences in this area, it was not unreasonable that Blackburn would substitute his judgment for Foster's and feel secure in his answers on recommendations. He performed a similar role with regard to queries from administrators in the system. When regional associates had a problem on their minds, Blackburn dealt with it and simply kept Foster informed.

In helping Foster achieve his goals, the deputy did not see himself as a "yes man," because Blackburn and the superintendent did argue over strategy and, to a lesser extent, over goals as well. During the weekly cabinet sessions Blackburn would sometimes argue with Foster to legitimize disagreement, in order to get the other members of the cabinet to do the same. Blackburn believed that Foster wanted his key aides to argue with him and to challenge his views. But it was not easy to get the other cabinet members to emulate his behavior. After all, the style of interaction between the superintendent and his deputy was based on a degree of trust which had not yet emerged in their relations with their new colleagues. In addition, because Foster did not have the time "to keep track of where things are in the system," a major part of Blackburn's job was to stay in touch with day-to-day routines, attending to those things that can be described as system-maintaining. This inside role helped Foster's deputy to carry out what he called his "particular task . . . [to] facilitate communication within the organization." As a result of his accessibility the system's staff came to him when they had questions on organizational routines. This was the division of labor which he and Foster sought.

THE SUPERINTENDENT'S PROTECTOR

An important part of the deputy's job is protecting the superintendent. Before coming to Oakland, Foster was concerned with the need for a man to "protect his flanks." In part, this was a racial problem, for Foster knew that his effectiveness would require an ability to meet the demands of the "stretched-out white folk" in Oakland. This did not mean that he avoided his white constituents. Rather, this division of labor was based on the shared belief of the two men that the superintendent's availability to non-white groups should be maximized. With the wide range of white voluntary associations in the city and the large number of requests for the superintendent to appear, they both knew that Foster could easily be overwhelmed. It was important to keep his schedule of speaking engagements sufficiently open to avoid turning down a black or other non-white community group's request. If one of the major, predominantly white civic groups invited the superintendent, however, he was almost certain to appear personally. Only on a few occasions did the deputy superintendent appear as Foster's representative at such meetings. By making himself accessible to the white community, Blackburn maintained that he was able to "keep track of the loose ends." That is, he was furthering the board-community relationships which were important to Foster's belief in the "community-centered" school. Blackburn knew that the superintendent was interested in the concerns of the white constituents, but he also recognized that the school district's executive simply lacked the time to give attention to everything.

When the deputy superintendent encountered rumblings of discontent, either in one of the meetings or through a telephone call, he often made a decision on the spot. This did not entail the risk which might be expected in circumstances where the two principal organizational executives did not know each other so well. Such risks were further reduced because Foster and Blackburn had essentially identical views on the nature of the tasks which they were undertaking. Nevertheless, the deputy was always careful to follow up his decision by personally informing the superintendent. He was especially attentive in this regard when the concerned group might schedule a subsequent appointment with Foster. In this way, Blackburn helped to keep Foster from being surprised or embarrassed if the question or issue were raised during the superintendent's discussion.

In view of the similarities in their beliefs and the fact that Foster and Blackburn had known each other for some time, it is interesting to note that the two men were not in frequent direct contact during the normal work day. Blackburn observed that he often saw the superintendent only when he "passes by my door." Nor was this compensated by a close social relationship outside the office. The two of them might chat briefly by phone, but even this was not frequent. Such conversations were usually restricted to information relevant to the subject of an evening meeting, or some critical event involving the schools and one of the many groups who were trying to get something from the superintendent.

Foster's deputy was not selected as a counterpoise to his own skills and values. Rather, Blackburn's selection was based on the superintendent's belief in the need for loyalty among his key advisers. This should not be taken to mean that the superintendent wanted his deputy to be a "yes-man." But because Foster wanted to "shake up the system," a second who shared his views and beliefs was more important to him than balance. He recognized, moreover, that his range of responsibilities as the superintendent of schools would not allow him to give his personal attention to all facets of those innovations which successful implementation would require. In addition Foster believed that some risks would have to be taken to institute the changes he wanted in the public schools. Blackburn had already shown that he, too, was willing to take risks in changing an organization. Willingness to accept risk, buttressed by personal loyalty to the leader and the experience of working together, made Blackburn a logical choice. While a handpicked deputy such as Blackburn can be of great help, the fact remained that he, too, was an outsider and could become a victim of ignorance. To help minimize the ignorance problem, the new leader sought to find insiders for his "core" group.

AN INSIDE TALENT HUNT

In his search for a leadership core, Foster, as I have stated above, followed a race-conscious selection policy. Such a criterion made sense because of public expectations and, most importantly, because Foster believed in his own "salt and pepper" rule. At the same time he was forced to consider other criteria. The leadership core would have to consist of individuals who could help Foster achieve *his* goals. Could they meet the tests of greater community involvement in school affairs? Would they be able to function in a decentralized organization? How would they adapt to a system-wide scheme of "management objectives" and its corollary of PPBS? What about increasing the responsibility of some men and decreasing that of others; would this create problems for Foster by engendering morale problems among the core group? These are just some of the questions which went through Foster's mind as he settled in. Each of these questions was directly related to the goals he wished to pursue, the "doable" policies which he had in mind for the Oakland public schools.

Foster had already indicated his willingness—indeed, his intention—to change by convincing the board to hire Price-Waterhouse. No one knew exactly what the management firm would report to Foster nor when Foster would act on the report once it was completed. And when he was questioned about his own plans for the school system, Foster would always put off answering with the response that "nothing was planned until after the Price-Waterhouse study was completed." But by the time this document was made public, Foster had already communicated its most salient recommendations through various public speaking engagements and in conversations or formal presentations to the staff, although neither group seemed to connect his remarks to the anticipated report.

THE BEGINNING OF STRUCTURAL CHANGE

With the formal acceptance of the Price-Waterhouse recommendations by the Board of Education on 23 September 1970, Foster began in earnest to institute change in the Oakland public schools. His first move was to get his own team together in cabinet. Where would he find the men?

Most public organizations are constrained to look among present organizational members to fill senior staff positions. This constraint has two sources: (1) urban public bureaucracies seldom have the kind of resource flexibility which is needed for an executive search; and (2) the norms of these bureaucracies create expectations that posts just below that of the chief executive will go to "insiders." Superintendent Foster's problem in selecting his team members could have been handled by leaving the inherited cabinet intact. But he knew that to do so would have told his constituency and the board that even under Foster it would continue to be "business as usual" in the Oakland public schools. Nevertheless, he was also aware that his organization was in violation of John W. Gardner's first rule on how to prevent "organization dry rot," which states that "the organization must have an effective program for the recruitment . . . of talent."[12] Moreover, the schools' political executive, like many other leaders of urban bureaucracies, could not afford the political costs of bringing in the schools' top men from outside. There are several reputed advantages to bringing in key executives from outside:

1. It obviates the delay incident to the long period of training necessary for the development of administrators within the service.
2. It eliminates the uncertainty as to the outcome that obtains when a position of large responsibilities is filled by promotion from one of lesser responsibilities.
3. It acts as an effective stimulus to the organization through the introduction of desirable "new blood."
4. It serves to counteract the tendency, usually more pronounced

12. John W. Gardner, "How to Prevent Organization Dry Rot," *Harper's Magazine*, October 1965, p. 20.

in the older organizations, to operate in accordance with the established though antiquated routine.

5. It brings into an organization the results of experience gained in different and possibly more highly developed fields of administration.[13]

While these advantages may all be real, there are legitimate objections which can be raised. Stockberger mentions one which is appropriate here:

Not infrequently a new incumbent of a high administrative position finds himself embarrassed by the necessity of calling upon more experienced subordinates, familiar with the technique of procedure, to instruct him in the methods to be followed if hopeless entanglements are to be avoided and looked-for ends are to be attained.[14]

When Foster kept his inherited cabinet intact he also accepted the risk of this embarrassment.

PRICE-WATERHOUSE PROPOSES,
FOSTER DISPOSES

In September 1970, barely three months after Marcus Foster became superintendent of schools, Price-Waterhouse, Inc., the management consultants whom he had hired, issued their report. The report recommended the creation of a variety of new positions to carry out the innovations Foster planned.[15] The positions of the assistant superintendents for instructional programs were abolished; they would be replaced by a single associate superintendent for educational development and services. Similarly, the business manager would be replaced by an associate superintendent for management systems. The budgeting function of the former business office was now to be taken over by a director of budget, who would be responsible to a new associate superintendent for planning, research and evaluation. This separation was based on the requirements of the proposed planning, programming and budgeting system, in which budgeting was viewed as an almost independent organizational task. An attempt to join the budget process with related organization activities was made

13. W. W. Stockberger, "The Need for Career Administrators," *The Annals of the American Academy of Political and Social Science* 189 (January 1937): 93.
14. Ibid., p. 94.
15. This section has benefited from several lengthy conversations with Elliot Medrich, a former staff member of the Oakland public schools.

by treating it as a part of planning. Price-Waterhouse also recommended the creation of three decentralized regions with approximately twenty thousand students per region. Each region would be headed by an associate superintendent. These three positions were totally new. With the exception of the director of budget, these positions would constitute the new cabinet.

The senior positions recommended by Price-Waterhouse involved small redefinitions and new titles for existing jobs. Predictably, a number of members of the organization believed that they had first call on some of these positions. Foster himself gave no indications of how he would fill the posts. Nothing was said publicly, nor did the superintendent communicate his intentions to the Board of Education. But Foster knew whom he wanted to fill which posts. By choice he did not invite applicants for the positions; instead he conducted a personal talent search among the system's staff. Foster had also decided that one member of the old cabinet did not figure in his plans for a new team. To avoid embarrassment to this individual, he chose an unusual approach and setting to make his choices known.

Early in October 1970 the superintendent's appointment secretary hand-delivered invitations to a special cabinet meeting to be held at the superintendent's home. When the meeting began, there was one new face among the regulars. Foster had decided on three associate superintendents for the regions proposed by Price-Waterhouse: one was to be the former director of personnel, another would be the assistant superintendent for urban educational services. Both of these men were black. The third—who was white (salt and pepper rule consistency)—was then principal of Oakland's newest and finest senior high school. The new position of associate superintendent for planning, research and evaluation was to be filled by the director of research, and the new post of associate superintendent for educational development and services would be taken over by the assistant superintendent for elementary instruction.

Only one position, that of associate superintendent for management systems, remained vacant. Benbow was not considered for this vacancy because he had already decided to retire within a few months, but he was present at this meeting. At the time of the meeting this position had already been advertised, applications had been received and some interviews conducted, but no choice had been made. During the discussion of this vacant post, Benbow argued in favor of one of his staff members but all of the other newly appointed associate superintendents argued even more strongly against him. And finally Benbow backed down. Unfortunately for this applicant, his reputation was not very good among other senior Oakland public schools staff members. The new cabinet then realized that there was no one in the system to whom this position should be given.

Foster was confident that once he had his associate superintendent for management systems his organization would be in a position to avoid a criticism voiced by John Gardner: "Most organizations have a structure . . . designed to solve problems that no longer exist."[16]

Foster controlled the options on the makeup of his leadership core. Because he moved quickly to select his new cabinet after the release of the Price-Waterhouse report there was little opportunity for others to attempt to influence his decisions. Thus internal competition for these elite positions did not materialize, because knowledge about Foster's intentions was restricted.

The superintendent did not have hard-and-fast criteria for the selection of his team. But he considered it essential that the members of his managerial elite be individuals with whom he could work. Foster's selection was actually begun before his arrival in Oakland. The written assessments of the organization and the proposals for change that Foster had requested from senior administrators while still in Philadelphia gave the superintendent some initial impressions of the range of choices. He was aided in making these early judgments by the informal summaries of several members of the Price-Waterhouse team.

Despite this intelligence, the superintendent's decisions were ultimately based on personal assessments of compatibility, loyalty and willingness to work toward his goals. The members of the new cabinet were handpicked and Foster believed they were thereby committed to him and his programs. This is not uncommon behavior for a chief executive. As Dean Mann has observed:

The President [too] is interested in staffing his administration with people personally and politically loyal to him, who will at the same time bring competence and support to the programs he espouses.[17]

16. Gardner, "Organization Dry Rot," p. 22.
17. Dean E. Mann, "The Selection of Federal Political Executives," *American Political Science Review* 58, no. 1 (March 1964): 82.

The use of personal, subjective criteria in choosing the regionals is understandable, if only because their jobs required less specifically technical or specialized knowledge. As Foster's "alter egos in the field" they, like the superintendent, were generalists.

Only in filling the management systems position did Foster set up a formal search, specifying the technical qualifications for the job. Again Foster turned to someone whose judgment he trusted for assistance. Price-Waterhouse, who had closely examined the business office as part of their management study, was deeply involved in the search for and screening of applicants for this important position.

Foster also sought to achieve other purposes by looking inside to fill most of his high-level appointments. The superintendent wanted to assure the principals that there was room for advancement in the system. In addition the new appointees were expected to forge a bond of interest based upon shared professional experiences in the Oakland public schools. And this interest was to be enhanced by linking older staff with the new leadership group who, after all, were products of the same system. Moreover, the black appointees were "naturally" expected to use their ties to Oakland's black community to further strengthen Foster's ability to lead the school system. As Theodore Lowi observed in discussing the appointment practices of some past mayors of New York City:

Communal or emotional identifications and rationalistic purposes are not incompatible. . . . As cohesive forces, the sense of common past and common destiny has served better than the best ideology, policies, and formal organizational structure.[18]

Most urban bureaucracies in the past decade have taken up this traditional practice and applied it on a somewhat broader scale to accommodate powerful new interest groups in their constituencies.

These appointments reflected Superintendent Foster's best judgments of the talents available to him. They represented something more as well. As Lowi noted for his New York City mayors:

Every appointment is a commitment. The pattern of appointments directly commits the Mayor to a stable or an unstable administration.

18. Theodore J. Lowi, *At the Pleasure of the Mayor* (New York: The Free Press, 1964), p. 128.

. . . Every type of appointment is also a *commitment in kind:* commitment to the appointees themselves and to [their] attributes.[19]

But the appointments signified even more than commitment; the superintendent was making his success hostage to the capability, skill, and loyalty of others whom he knew less well than his deputy. This is why Foster was so deeply involved in the selection of his associate superintendents. He knew what the risks were. If these selections turned out badly it would be his fault and would engender recriminations from those members of the organization who had been passed over. Should Foster's choices acquit themselves well, he was not likely to get much public credit, only the private satisfaction of knowing he had decided wisely. By casting the regional associates as his "alter egos" and by frequently reinforcing this characterization in public and private statements, the superintendent linked their identity with his own. Unfortunately, this identification was likely to be remembered more in adversity than in success.

Although Foster initially believed that his new cabinet would reduce the number of people reporting directly to the superintendent, he seemed to have accomplished just the opposite. Previously there had been five men reporting to the superintendent; now there were seven (including the deputy). Nevertheless, in practice it turned out that Foster did have fewer persons reporting to him directly, because the three regional associate superintendents were more frequently in contact with Blackburn than with Foster. Under the new cabinet structure only two men regularly reported directly to Foster: the deputy superintendent and the associate superintendent for planning, research and evaluation.[20]

Herbert Simon saw this kind of expansion of the executive organization as a paradox, as he wryly commented on the Hoover Commission's recommendations of 1937:

The . . . government is too large and complex to be controlled effectively by the President. We will remedy this [as the Hoover Commission recommended] by creating a new agency [BOB], thus increasing its size and complexity.[21]

19. Ibid., p. 181. Emphasis in original.
20. There was one other person who also reported directly to the superintendent: the coordinator of staff relations. This individual was also responsible for negotiations with the teachers organization. He was not a member of the cabinet.
21. Herbert A. Simon, "Staff and Management Controls," *The Annals of the American Academy of Political and Social Science* 292 (March 1954): 98-99.

Foster had a similar belief about the Oakland public schools, which he handled by appointing three associate superintendents for decentralized regions, thus adding to the complexity of his organization.

The superintendent's cabinet, and especially the regionals, did much to lighten Foster's decision load. Fewer decisions to make on day-to-day problems may give the political executive time to construct a more organizationally productive role, as Simon describes here:

An executive usually starts with a clean slate in a new organization, and gradually accumulates a host of routine "maintenance" activities. He must take steps periodically to free his time from these growing barnacles of programmed activity. Delegation is a continuing process—what is not delegatable this month, because it is important and novel, must and should be delegated next month because it has become routine. Few executives succeed in freeing themselves for nonprogrammed activity unless they give conscious thought to the means of doing it. There is a sort of "Gresham's Law" whereby routine drives out creative thinking. Unless the executive conscientiously allocates time to innovation, he will find ways to fritter away his time by absorbing it in routine.[22]

But in gaining a more productive role for himself, the superintendent inadvertently cast his "alter egos" in a very fragile role. In an effort to enhance their positions, the superintendent sought for ways to make regional responsibility a viable aspect of the school system's operations. Most frequently this has meant searching for money with which to respond to the regional associates' innovative program requests. As Blackburn once told the cabinet, the superintendent wanted these "three troops [to have] a few pennies and discretion to get some things going." Foster recognized that part of the problems the regional associates were facing stemmed from the fact that principals simply had not become accustomed to using the regional associate superintendents as contact points. They were used to calling directly on the central administration for information and aid.

The organizational elite is expected to operate as a cohesive

22. Herbert A. Simon, "The Decision Maker as Innovator," in *Concepts and Issues in Administrative Behavior*, ed. Sidney Mallick and Edward Van Ness (Englewood Cliffs, N.J.: Prentice-Hall, 1962), p. 68.

unit in accordance with the educational philosophy of the political executive. Foster became aware that a few cabinet members were having difficulty in grasping his philosophy. In some cases the superintendent thought his "people were simply on a different wave length and could not be brought around" to his way of thinking. But disagreement on broad questions of organizational policy need not produce conflict. He saw no real problems coming from a philosophical difference with his top men so long as they did not actively obstruct or otherwise damage his goals. If a leader could get this kind of behavioral consistency, Foster believed, it did not matter if there were differences of opinion. He thought it was enough for a leader to surround himself with "capable and trustworthy" top staff. Trust is an important ingredient in the decision to keep a man who disagrees in the leader's elite decisionmaking group. If he was assured of a member's overall loyalty, Superintendent Foster was not uncomfortable in giving him the freedom to act in his area of responsibility.

Marcus Foster, as we have seen, did not want to be involved in day-to-day operations; that was a staff responsibility. Besides, it was too time-consuming for a leader who placed more importance on the need to build support for his organization. The superintendent took the traditional option of delegating, buttressed by board preference and legitimized by the Price-Waterhouse report. But Foster's willingness to stay out of operational areas which were the responsibility of his associate superintendents did not extend to the point of relinquishing all decision-making authority. Thus, although the superintendent resembled Franklin D. Roosevelt in his use of conflict to clarify issues, his style of reaching a decision was more akin to that of Eisenhower, who, says Fenno,

likes to reach his conclusions by talking out his thoughts rather than brooding. [Eisenhower] likes to take in by ear all that he can. This means that he will pass problems around for discussions . . . , listen carefully to their debates, and use them as a sounding board. . . . He is apt, in other words, to do his thinking in the presence of others, in a group meeting.[23]

But this style did not apply across the board. Early in his tenure Foster encountered some difficulty in getting the ideas of his

23. Fenno, *The President's Cabinet*, p. 41.

cabinet members in areas where he had already expressed an opinion. They were not willing to "push back," as he called it, against his ideas and comments. In part, of course, this was simply a consequence of his newness coupled with the inherited cabinet's uncertainty about what he wanted to do. The problem persisted even after the superintendent had put his team together. Blackburn saw that Foster was not getting what he wanted in the way of discussion and would often play the devil's advocate just to encourage others to challenge the superintendent. But even this legitimation of dissent seldom provoked full discussion of Foster's overall policies. The lack of debate over his innovations stemmed partly from the fact that the superintendent never presented them as matters for discussion. Indeed the best opportunity to raise contrary views came at the meeting in Foster's home where the members of his cabinet learned of their selection. Still, it was clear to those attending that accepting the new posts implied a commitment to the superintendent's proposed changes in the organization.

A key feature of Foster's leadership of cabinet was his avoidance of operational matters, for he believed that once a program or policy was operational the leader should get out of the way. The political executive also needs to keep in mind the fact that no matter how strongly he may hold a particular policy preference, it cannot be accomplished overnight. He has to give it time. And as Bruce Headey observed in a study of British ministers, "It is up to the Prime Minister to find the right man [sic] for the departments, and let them stay in office long enough to make a worthwhile contribution."[24]

But how could Foster lead his cabinet? We have already seen that he avoided operations and routines because these were considered to be staff functions. In addition, we have seen that Foster's particular skills lay in developing a permissive environment for innovation in his organization's structure and processes. And despite an awareness of the instrumental value of some of his acts for his own political resources, Foster had to adapt his concern for the affective dimension of leadership in dealing with his constituents to meet his need to get things done by his senior

24. Bruce Headey, "What Makes for a Strong Minister," *New Society*, 8 October 1970, p. 627.

staff.[25] We saw some of this concern for affect in Superintendent Foster's dealings with the principals after he introduced the new principal selection process. With the members of his cabinet, Foster also tried to instill something of himself and his style in attempting to get them to act as his alter egos.

The superintendent's commitment to his own vision of where the school system should be going so clearly dominated the cabinet that it is difficult to imagine these men raising objections. Moreover, it is somewhat unfair to expect that they should have done so, because they were all weighted down by the pressures of getting started in their new positions. Here Superintendent Foster was in much the same position as that of the board members when they hired him. Despite the written assessments they had sent to him in Philadelphia and the judgments of his Price-Waterhouse consultants, Foster did not really know these men and their capabilities. He and Blackburn were convinced that the leadership core would be committed and loyal. Their ability to successfully implement Foster's innovations, however, was not yet known.

CONTROL OF THE CABINET PROCESS
IS NOT ALWAYS IMPORTANT

While Dr. Foster was an active participant in cabinet deliberations, his role frequently took on the characteristics of a participant observer. His greatest involvement was normally limited to the preparation of the board's agenda. He tried to make sure that any unanswered questions from previous board meetings would be answered, or at least that an answer was being prepared. He made certain, moreover, that he knew who was responsible for preparing the response should he need to be "backstopped" at the next board meeting.

The superintendent was also especially attentive to issues raised by the associate superintendent for planning, research and evaluation, because they generally have budgetary implications. And

25. Some suggestive comments on leadership pertinent to Foster's efforts are provided in an early work by Woodrow Wilson. See Woodrow Wilson, *Leaders of Men*, ed. T. H. Vail Motter (Princeton: Princeton University Press, 1952), pp. 23-24. See also the insightful discussion of Mao's attempt to transfer his style and understanding to his subordinates in John W. Lewis, "Leader, Commissar and Bureaucrat: The Chinese Political System in the Last Days of the Revolution," *Journal of International Affairs* 24, no. 1 (1970): 58.

the budget was the other area of administration in which Foster got closely involved. Involvement meant, however, that he paid close attention and usually asked more questions than he did in other areas of administration. Typically he would follow the recommendations of the associate superintendent in charge of that area.

During the work sessions for budget preparation the superintendent's presence was strongly felt. He had questions for everyone in the cabinet on the implications of particular budget decisions. The superintendent's personal involvement in budget cutting was essential to the associate superintendent for planning, research and evaluation, who once pointed out that he and two of the regionals had sat down in an attempt to make some initial decision about cuts but "nothing happened." When Foster became personally involved decisions were made quickly. This associate believed that "without Foster, each associate superintendent would act in a very protective way toward his area." This observation also raises another issue with regard to the behavior of the cabinet in decisionmaking. Each of the members can be regarded as a department head with roles analogous to the president's cabinet secretaries. And as Richard F. Fenno, Jr., commented of the latter,

in view of the department head's problems of success and survival . . . he may deliberately assume postures and adopt positions that are department-oriented, and which may not accord with presidential desires.[26]

For Foster, however, this possibility did not loom as a risk to his leadership. He believed that casting the regional associate superintendents as his alter egos would bring them to share his views and act in ways that were best for the organization.

The cabinet amounted functionally to what Barnard has called the "informal executive organization." Its members were responsible for the "communication of intangible facts, opinions, suggestions, suspicions, that cannot pass through formal channels without raising issues calling for decisions."[27] Indeed the regionals found the chief value of the cabinet to be the regular opportunities the meetings gave them to share concerns and ideas of mutual interest.

26. Fenno, *The President's Cabinet,* p. 231.
27. There is an interesting discussion of this point in Sarason, *The Creation of Settings,* pp. 190-93.

Sometimes, however, the regionals could successfully "push back" on the superintendent by presenting a "front" on a particular matter. It was not necessary for all of them to want the same thing. The most effective argument they had was their need to be legitimated and to be seen as effective by the principals and the public. Even in a constrained financial state they knew that Foster would usually respond positively if their request was reasonable and made good "pedagogical sense." The superintendent wanted and needed them to be successful. On their efficacy depended his own.

The new cabinet did not represent a complete break with past organizational practices. Under Foster, as before, it continued to be the decisionmaking body of the organization. Its principal new feature was more symbolic than substantive: now there were blacks in prominent executive positions.

Yet in combination with decentralization (to be discussed in the following chapter) the new cabinet provided an improvement in the intelligence-gathering function of the school system. The presence of the regionals in the cabinet was expected to counter a problem described by Harold Wilensky:

... if intelligence is scattered throughout subordinate units, too many officials and experts with too much specialized information may engage in dysfunctional competition, may delay decisions while they warily consult each other, and may distort information as they pass it up.[28]

By simultaneously being "in the field" and members of the organizational elite, the three regionals would be in a better position to acquire useful intelligence which could be fed into the decisionmaking process.

The cabinet device was best suited to dealing with organizational routines. It gave Foster some insight into the day-to-day operations of the school district. The cabinet also helped to resolve some of the small problems which inevitably arise in a complex public bureaucracy. But the superintendent's men were not used to clarify major policy issues. The superintendent did not explicitly conceive of their individual or collective roles as providing him with advice on policy. And what is more, the associate superintendents made few attempts to act as policy

28. Harold Wilensky, *Organizational Intelligence* (New York: Basic Books, 1967), p. 58.

advisors to the superintendent. Perhaps if they had done so Superintendent Foster's planned innovations might have fared better.

5

Decentralization:
The Reform of the Organization

Superintendent Foster, like most organizational leaders, was confronted by serious disparities as he planned his changes. For this reason, and for others not so tangible, his policies for change may be characterized, following Choucri and North, "as operating to minimize, or close, one or a combination of three fundamental types of gap":

1. a gap between resources that are "needed" or demanded and those actually available;
2. a gap between expectation and the reality that materializes;
3. a gap between one's own resources or growth rate and those of a competitor or rival.[1]

The recognition of these gaps forced Foster to launch his innovations within the resource constraints he found in the Oakland public schools when he took office. However, neither a new leadership style nor community involvement had required the use of "hard" resources. And neither of these changes caused substantive alterations in the structure of Foster's organization.

Even the new cabinet had cost little. By selecting mostly insiders for the leadership core the salaries to go with their new positions required only modest increases. As the superintendent

1. Nazli Choucri and Robert C. North, "Dynamics of International Conflict," *World Politics* 24, supplement (Spring 1972).

proceeded with his plans to decentralize the school system, he continued to act as though structural changes could also be achieved at minimal cost.

For the superintendent decentralization was a structural and not a cyclical change. This distinction has been cogently stated by Theodore Lowi in the following terms:

Operationally, cyclical change is simply a "blip" in a secular trend, a clear, discontinuous departure from the established pattern and then a return shortly thereafter to the established pattern. Conversely, a *structural* change is one that departs from the pattern and does not later return to it; i.e., a departure that begins a new pattern.[2]

In combination with community involvement through the Master Plan Citizens Committee, decentralization would permanently redefine the relationship between the organization and its environment.

Structural change, however, also implies value changes among an organization's members. The creation of an appropriate value base for structural changes is a primary responsibility of the political executive. Foster's first attempt to instill new values came in the form of community involvement, and decentralization was treated as an extension of that effort.

The school system's leader readily accepted the obligation to make his values those of his organization as well. As Philip Selznick reminds us:

Truly accepted values must infuse the organization at many levels, affecting the perspectives and attitudes of personnel, the relative importance of staff activities, the distribution of authority, relations with outside groups, and many other matters.[3]

Despite his belief that the board had given him a mandate to change the organization, Foster knew he had to sell his ideas. This is a further illustration of why Foster maintained such a rugged schedule of speaking engagements during his first months in office. This kind of behavior was essential, he said, "in order to get your philosophy in place and try to bring people around to your view when you don't have very much time to make changes." He continued, "You have to say it and do it, and then

2. Theodore Lowi, *At the Pleasure of the Mayor* (New York: The Free Press, 1964), p. 191.
3. Philip Selznick, *Leadership and Administration* (New York: Harper & Row, 1957), p. 26.

talk about what you did. . . . It's necessary to get your people [your staff], especially your principals, to internalize your philosophy of what the system should be doing."

As leaders attempt to implement changes in their organizations it is usually assumed that the results will be for the better. Yet there are numerous cases where these outcomes have not been beneficial. A study of an effort to change the YMCA some years ago expressed the point quite well:

> Change does not necessarily solve problems. It may result only in exchanging one set of problems for another. Change is not necessarily progress. Change may result in deterioration. Change is not inherently valuable. Why changes are made, how they are made, is as important as whether changes are made.[4]

Each of these caveats applied to the changes which Foster introduced in Oakland. Moreover, there is a further question related to organizational change which is only infrequently asked: how much change can an ongoing organization accept? It is not merely an issue of quantity, it is also one of timing. An organization or its component units may be able to tolerate substantial change if no single operational unit or level is required to adopt, or adapt to, many changes in a brief span of time.

The broad extent of decentralization already found in public school systems illustrates this aspect of the general problem. The Oakland Unified School District already had approximately ninety decentralized units, each with a manager (principal) who possessed considerable autonomy. The more Foster talked of the need to empower the local schools, that is, reallocate the amount of authority within his organization, the greater the likelihood of demands to make resources available to give effect to that authority. Unless steps were taken to meet those demands for resources a crisis of expectations was almost sure to emerge among the new recipients.

The dilemma facing the superintendent as he attempted to fulfill this promise to make the school system responsive is an old one in the literature on organizations:

4. Ray Johns, *Confronting Organizational Change* (New York: The Association Press, 1963), p. 16.

Despite sharp distinction in purpose, a common problem in all [large, complex formal organizations] is the dichotomy between the pressure for *centralization* of authority to assure corporate integrity, and the countering pressure for *decentralization* in administration to secure *efficiency* through ready response to diverse conditions and human motivations.[5]

The use of the efficiency criterion to measure organizational effectiveness has an extensive "half-life" in the literature on administration. Nevertheless, it is a notion which carries at least two distinct meanings. On the one hand, efficiency, in the minds of those whose tax bills support public organizations, is equated with cost reductions. Almost invariably members of the public assume that this type of efficiency can be obtained with no loss in service. More recently notions of efficiency have been reformulated to mean that the delivery of services to clients could be improved if the responsible organizations would set their objectives in measurable terms. If this is done, so the argument goes, rational allocations of scarce resources can be made, consistent with the achievement of stated, though not unanimously agreed-upon, goals.

INSTITUTE CHANGE,
EVEN WHEN IGNORANT OF CONTEXT

Organizational leaders enter new settings with varying degrees of ignorance. Depending on their own orientation to risk, several strategies are open to them. One of these is to proceed cautiously and slowly with regard to the introduction of change. Or a new leader may move ahead quickly, hoping to capitalize on the initial atmosphere of uncertainty which characterizes his arrival. The Oakland schools' new political executive adopted a strategy combining both of these approaches. He realized that moving too quickly in the face of inadequate knowledge might jeopardize the success of some later policy initiatives, but at the same time he wanted to demonstrate that there was indeed a new man in office who had definite ideas about what public education should do in response to the demands which had been raised in the past several years.

5. Helen Baker and Robert R. France, *Centralization and Decentralization in Industrial Relations* (Princeton: Industrial Relations Section, Princeton University Press, 1954), p. 5, quoted in Bernard H. Baum, *Decentralization of Authority in a Bureaucracy* (Englewood Cliffs, N.J.: Prentice-Hall, 1961), p. 36.

Studies of leadership frequently call attention to the fact that leaders often fail because they don't know what they want. With decentralization the superintendent knew what he did *not* want. Foster studiously avoided anything which might have cast the issue of decentralization as an effort to integrate Oakland's schools. Both he and the board recognized that any talk about integration would involve the schools in a major controversy with the public. In addition, several of the board members believed that this was the one subject which was certain to force them into opposing the superintendent. Integration of the Oakland schools was really a moot point, for the school population was almost 75 percent non-white. Meaningful integration under such circumstances was simply not feasible. And what is more, there was no substantial community sentiment—black or white—pressing for school integration.[6]

There are two principal reasons to explain why integration did not become a public issue in administrative decentralization: (1) the superintendent emphasized that attendance boundaries were not to be disturbed by the change; and (2) he had no strong pro-integration motivations which might have intruded on the plans to make three regions out of the district. But decentralization was still a difficult task for the research division to whom the superintendent assigned the responsibility for developing the plans for his "mini-districts." Perhaps more clearly than with either of his other innovations, however, Foster had a specific idea of what decentralization was to do and a definite rationale for its adoption.

Foster insisted that each of the three regions was to be a smaller version of the total school district. Each regional associate superintendent was to have a scaled-down version of what the superintendent faced on a daily basis. The three regions were to be the same size (approximately 20,000 students); each was to reflect the

6. But see the list of variables associated with pressures to decentralize in a sample of twenty-nine cities in George R. LaNoue and Bruce L. R. Smith, *The Politics of School Decentralization* (Lexington, Mass.: D. C. Heath, 1973). pp. 28-29, table 3-1. There is, of course, ample evidence of cities in which school integration was a major question of public policy. For examples of this literature see Robert L. Crain and David Street, "School Desegregation and School Decision-Making," in *Educating an Urban Population*, ed. Marilyn Gittell (Beverly Hills: Sage Publications, 1967), pp. 136-54; and Robert L. Crain, *The Politics of School Desegregation* (Chicago: Aldine Publishing Co., 1968).

racial and ethnic makeup of the overall district; and—the most troublesome criterion—each region was to be approximately equal in terms of academic achievement as measured by the most recent standardized achievement test and SES levels for students from families receiving welfare assistance.

The final plan was selected from eight alternatives prepared by the research division. On the whole they satisfied the superintendent's criteria, except that middle and upper class Oaklanders (black and white) almost seemed to get their own sub-district in the southeastern section of the city.

Cabinet consideration of the eight plans for decentralization of the school district took approximately twelve days. Throughout the deliberations in cabinet Foster continued to maintain that the idea of the microcosm was based on his intention to regard the three regional associate superintendents as his alter egos. Consequently it was necessary that their regional responsibilities be a reflection of Foster's responsibilities for the total school district.

THE EIGHT PROPOSALS FOR DECENTRALIZATION

PLAN I:

This plan got the most positive initial response. It had good racial balance, and flatland and hill schools were reasonably distributed in each of the three regions presented. This plan also illustrated the difficulties which would be faced in meeting the criteria set by Foster. It highlighted the problem of noncontiguity and also starkly portrayed the maldistribution of wealth throughout the city. Of course, most citizens had a good idea of which sections of the city were wealthy, but the cabinet realized that it would be a political blunder if the decentralization scheme appeared to reflect city income patterns.

PLAN II:

Did not have geographic districts, although it portrayed racial distribution that was approximately what Foster sought. And although the total number of schools per region was about right, total enrollments were out of line.

PLAN III:

The members of the cabinet viewed this alternative as an extreme. It had good enrollment distribution but the racial mix was poor, as was the distribution of schools throughout the regions. Basically, Plan III failed to meet Foster's criterion of reproducing the overall system.

PLAN IV:

This was acceptable on enrollment, but the distribution of schools was unsatisfactory. Moreover, Plan IV did not adequately respond to the issue of racial distribution.

PLAN V:

Like Plan III it was an extreme. It failed on enrollment, the number of schools, and racial distribution.

PLAN VI:

This was for all practical purposes ignored. However it did show that most of the high-achieving schools would be in one region of the city.

PLAN VII:

Attempted to spread the affluence of the city throughout the proposed regions. It was believed that this could be done if the plan focused on the junior high schools, but it turned out to be more difficult than expected to meet the other microcosm criteria. Using the junior high schools would have seriously disrupted existing school attendance boundaries.

PLAN VIII:

Would have assigned part of Oakland to different areas and modified the existing feeder plans for the high schools. This one was also rejected because the administration would be liable to charges of desegregating the district under the guise of decentralization had it been adopted.

The first plan, although it had received the greatest positive response initially, came in for some serious criticism by virtually everyone in the cabinet. The criticism was largely based on the fact that, as one associate put it, "Skyline has administrative unity and articulation that no other area has. . . . Plan I continues Skyline High School as a bastion of bigotry." Skyline High School, the showcase high school in Oakland, had a gerrymandered attendance area which had caused a major flap in the city of Oakland when it was developed. The attendance area for the school was long and narrow, running along the top of the hills behind the city, so that only those who lived in the Oakland hills, mainly wealthy whites, could send their children there. This plan naturally angered a large number of Oakland black and other non-white citizens, but it also angered a substantial portion of other middle and upper middle class citizens in Oakland who lived in the foothills. Their residential area was just outside the attendance area of Skyline High School. The board lost considerable public support as a result of its decision to draw the boundary lines for the school in the extremely restrictive fashion which they adopted. Notwithstanding the problems with the high visibility of Skyline and its tendency to reawaken old and somewhat painful memories, Plan I—which left the Skyline attendance area intact—was the only one which could get a consensus. When the vote was finally taken on the proposals, Plan I was the obvious winner with six votes. The makeup of the three regions as finally adopted by the cabinet is presented in Charts 1 to 4.

Chart 1. Enrollments

	5,000	10,000	15,000	20,000	25,000
Region 1. Castlemont and Oakland Technical areas				20,559	30 schools
Region 2. McClymonds, Oakland, Dewey and Grant areas			19,843		30 schools
Region 3. Castlemont and Skyline areas				22,757	30 schools
	5,000	10,000	15,000	20,000	25,000

Number of students

The failure to get unanimous support for this plan resulted from Blackburn's disapproval. He was unwilling to compromise on the demographic criteria. The source of the deputy superintendent's concern about Plan I can be seen in Chart 4 dealing with "students from welfare families." But the plan which left Skyline intact also was the fairest in terms of meeting the superintendent's insistence on giving each region a "microcosm" of the city's schools. The cabinet also believed that some of the SES achievement disparities would be mitigated by the larger size of the region containing Skyline High School.

Chart 2. Ethnic Characteristics

Region 1. Castlemont and Oakland Technical areas				
B 54%	SS 12%	A 6%	W 26%	-0 2%

Region 2. McClymonds, Oakland, Dewey and Grant areas				
B 56%	SS 8%	A 8%	W 26%	-0 1%

Region 3. Castlemont and Skyline areas				
B 60%	SS 5%	A	W 32%	0 1%

Black = Black, SS = Spanish Surname, A = Asian, W = White, O = Other
Source: Research Department, Oakland Unified School District.

Chart 3. Reading Achievement

Below National Norms	Above National Norms
Region 1	Castlemont and Oakland Technical
67%	33%
Region 2	McClymonds, Oakland, Dewey and Grant
64%	36%
Region 3	Castlemont and Skyline
62%	38%

80 70 60 50 40 30 20   20 30 40 50 60 70 80
Percent   Percent

Throughout their discussion of the plans for decentralization Foster frequently had to remind his associate superintendents that he was not interested in strict geographic regions. What he planned for the Oakland schools was "not a device for changing children" in the district. The purpose of regional decentralization was to reorganize "middle management." That is, to improve the management of the schools, especially in the areas of delivering services to the individual schools.

The superintendent also had to make certain that his plan would answer some concerns of the Board of Education. The

Chart 4. Students from Welfare Families

Percent of Students

| 0 | 5 | 10 | 15 | 20 | 25 | 30 | 35 | 40 |

Region 1. Castlemont and Oakland Technical areas	30%	
Region 2. McClymonds, Oakland, Dewey and Grant areas	32%	District Average = 28%
Region 3. Castlemont and Skyline areas	21%	

| 0 | 5 | 10 | 15 | 20 | 25 | 30 | 35 | 40 |

Percent of Students

board members were uneasy about the implications for Oakland of a legislative plan to reorganize the Los Angeles school district. Although the Los Angeles enrollment was more than twelve times the size of Oakland's, the board feared that the legislature might impose a similar plan on them. The board members' anxieties had not been calmed by an earlier report from their legislative representative in Sacramento. He told the board in August 1970, three months before Foster's plan was received:

It is my opinion that SB-242 has little or no immediate implication for Oakland. There has been no interest in decentralization of the Oakland district . . . by any member of our legislative delegation and, so far as I can recall, very little from the community. I do not think that anyone in Sacramento will take an interest in decentralizing Oakland unless there are substantial indications from within the community that decentralization is desired. . . . I attended most of the extensive hearings on SB-242 and at no time was there any direct testimony from community groups in support of the bill. On the contrary, there were many witnesses from community groups, P.T.A., NAACP, and others who appeared in opposition to the bill.[7]

Still, the Board of Education continued to think that decentralization somehow implied desegregation/integration. The board's uneasiness made it easier for Foster to sell his plan on the three criteria of racial heterogeneity, achievement and SES. Instead of a desegregation plan, with its potential for producing controversy, decentralization was couched in technical, educational policy terms.

7. Memorandum to Marcus A. Foster from Arthur C. Pokorny, 27 August 1970, pp. 2-3. From school district files.

THE BOARD DOES NOT CLOSELY EXAMINE
"TECHNICAL" POLICY QUESTIONS

By late December 1970 Superintendent Foster was ready to announce his first structural change in the school district. The
superintendent, as we have seen, moved very deliberately with
decentralization. He carefully delineated the scope of the plan
and restricted the number of actors who were involved in the
deliberations and planning for this innovation. Although the
regional associate superintendents had been selected in October,
Foster withheld any announcement to the board and the public
until the regions themselves were also created. He wanted to
submit the names and regional decentralization to the board in a
package. If the announcements were made separately, he believed, it might stir demands for community involvement similar
to that which was practiced in principal selection. The superintendent felt, however, that since these were *his* men—his "alter
egos"—he had to make certain that he could work with them.
Because he was strongly committed to the notion of accountability, the community could hold him accountable for these key
appointments, but after the fact. Moreover, the decentralization
of the district would be the first major test of board support for
their new superintendent of schools. Foster anticipated opposition, for he told his cabinet, "They've got to buck me on it!" The
superintendent knew that a decentralization policy was a matter
which should have been discussed with the board before he acted.
By presenting the total scheme at one time, however, the superintendent hoped to give the board members little room for questioning and criticism. To do otherwise, he feared, would take
time and could delay adoption. And a delay at this point would
have led to a delay in the move to PPBS which was yet to come.
With everything in order the superintendent presented the plan
to the board in executive session, as it involved personnel.

In his covering memorandum, Dr. Foster specified the rationale for administrative decentralization:

Among the major recommendations of the Price-Waterhouse report,
Recommendations to Improve Management Effectiveness, was the decentralization of some of the management. Price-Waterhouse proposed
the creation of three regional organizations, each headed by an associate superintendent, in order to enhance the management effectiveness
of the district. It is important to note that these regions are intended to

be administrative rather than political entities. Under the regional organization plan now being proposed the three Regional Associate Superintendents will report to the Deputy Superintendent and will function as the Superintendent's personal representatives. They will have administrative authority over the principals and will be primarily concerned with achieving measurable progress toward District goals in each of the schools of the region.[8]

He emphasized the important features of his proposal, especially those which would allay any fears about integration and desegregation:

1. FULL RANGE OF PERFORMANCE AND POPULATION IN EACH REGION:

Each regional Associate Superintendent will give leadership to a group of schools representing a microcosm of education in Oakland. The student populations and communities in each region will reflect the cosmopolitan nature of the entire district. . . .

2. NO BOUNDARY CHANGES:

No school boundary or school feeder plans have been changed from their present designations.

3. THREE EQUAL-SIZED REGIONS:

The numbers of schools and enrollments are approximately equal for each region.

4. FEEDER PLAN ARTICULATION:

Kindergarten through high school feeder systems have generally been kept within a single region. There are, of course, exceptions in two main instances: (a) some elementary and/or junior high schools send students to more than one higher-level school; (b) two junior high schools (Havenscourt and Bret Harte) and their feeder elementary schools have been assigned to regions containing the high school where many, but not the majority, of their students attend in order to bring about a balance in the enrollments and demographic characteristics of the regions.

5. DIRECT ADMINISTRATIVE CONTACTS:

Administrative proximity rather than geographic proximity was the chief criterion for assigning the school clusters to the respective regions.

8. Oakland Unified School District, Office of the Superintendent, "Plan for the Creation of Administrative Regions," 15 December 1971 (Memorandum to the Board of Education).

6. IMMEDIATE DEVELOPMENT OF REGIONAL ADMINISTRATIVE UNITS:

Under this plan it will be possible to establish and organize regional administrative units. The Associate Superintendents and their staffs in these units will gain experience in dealing with a full range of needs and programs and, thereby, will be ready to assume the responsibilities which evolve from the Master Planning that is now in process as well as in Planning, Programming and Budgeting System procedures that must be implemented under state and local mandates.[9]

The Board of Education readily accepted the superintendent's rationale for decentralization. They were satisfied that their chief executive had done a professionally competent job. But the board was concerned about the personnel aspects of the plan—the associate superintendents for the regions.

In spite of Foster's effort to present decentralization as a package, the board made it into two separate issues. The preparation of the regions was a technical matter and they relied upon the superintendent to exercise his best judgment in submitting a recommendation for board action. On the question of naming key administrative personnel, however, the board members believed they had a right, if not a duty, to be involved in the selection process. Besides, they believed themselves the equal of the superintendent in making wise personnel decisions.

Dr. Foster may not have had to suffer a defeat on his associate superintendent's appointments had it not been for a characteristic of his style in dealing with the board. The superintendent did not believe in getting too close to members of the board. This also meant that he sometimes did not discuss his intentions with them privately.

His predecessor, Dr. Benbow, however, believed that "lots of times the superintendent knows what board members will do because he knows them well from . . . frequent contact." When he had been in office he had spent a "great deal of time in telephone conversations" on school business. "It is a useful way," he said, "for the superintendent to line up votes," prior to formal board presentation. He described the practice of an earlier superintendent, who would assign three members of the board to him (when Benbow was business manager) to line up their votes. The

9. Ibid.

superintendent would handle the other four. Had Foster adopted a similar practice he would have learned early on that some members of the board were opposed to one of his nominees.

CRACKS IN RACIAL SOLIDARITY

One of the black administrators designated as a regional associate superintendent was dissatisfied with the tentative assignment which he had been given. During cabinet discussions he argued strongly that each of the three should be assigned to a region in which he had direct experience and community contacts. Although the argument was reasonable, the superintendent wanted to confound those who would have expected such assignments. Foster reasoned that making the appointments to regions where the individuals would feel most "at home" would have meant leaving the white appointee in the region where he had been a principal. To the superintendent this would have been interpreted as "Oakland doing the same old thing." He wanted to make sure that with decentralization the schools would be doing things differently. Moreover, making an unexpected assignment of this type would give further evidence to observers that Foster controlled the initiatives.

In an attempt to force the superintendent to change his assignment the newly designated associate superintendent encouraged some of his supporters in the black community to lobby for him with Foster. Very shortly after this began, the two black board members also learned of the private meeting at which the cabinet assignments were made. They were upset because Foster, a fellow black, had not taken them into his confidence. The superintendent had treated them as board members.

The problem for Foster stemmed, however, from the fact that his choice was closer to the black activists than to the black "establishment" whom the two board members represented. But they based their objections on the limited administrative experience of Foster's choice. They pointed out that he had no service as a principal and consequently was not likely to handle the sensitive position of associate superintendent properly. In making this argument they ignored the fact that the individual was at the time responsible for compensatory education programs in the schools. These federally financed programs accounted for approximately ten percent of the school district's annual budget. And, of course, he was the highest ranking black administrator (assistant superintendent) when Foster took over.

In any case, the two board members did not absolutely veto Foster's recommendation, but they expressed such strong reservations that Foster "got the message." In addition, the white majority took their cue on the issue from their black colleagues. The board was willing to accept all of the superintendent's recommendations for decentralization and the other cabinet members, but only two of the regional appointments. Foster was unwilling to accept this arrangement. He elected to take the total package back for further consideration. Foster was trying to protect his options by making it appear that he was reexamining the entire plan.

Foster was certain that had he wanted, he could have forced a decision and got a 4-3 majority in his favor, but this margin would have been too thin and he believed it would have posed problems for his future relationships with the board members who voted in the minority. The superintendent could not afford, so early in his tenure, to provoke stern opposition from the two black board members and the one liberal on the board, who would very likely have voted with them. This might have jeopardized some of his other plans. The issue of that one appointment might also have threatened Foster's relations with some key members of his constituency, as one of the most important politically active blacks in the city was a friend of the two black board members and a former board member himself. As a result he withdrew the appointment and went outside the district to find the third regional associate superintendent. The outsider (also black) came from a neighboring school district. Moreover, he had more classroom and school site administrative experience than Foster's original nominee. The board approved his selection. Although the superintendent had expected the board to "buck him" on the decentralization plan, the defeat was an embarrassment to Foster. Nevertheless, the second of Foster's planned innovations was under way. But a decentralization plan becomes a different order of problem when implementation begins.

WHAT CAN YOU DECENTRALIZE?

The newly appointed regional associate superintendents were confronted by substantial problems as they sought to create viable organizational roles for themselves. Almost immediately these three executives keenly felt the lack of resources.

As part of the overall effort to bring services closer to those who needed them, some psychological services personnel had been assigned to the regional offices. A year after this arrangement came into effect the regionals found themselves embroiled in a dispute with the director of special education, that is, education of variously handicapped students. The heads of the regions wanted to enhance the decentralized arrangement by acquiring more of the special education services for their regional offices. In a memorandum to Foster they argued:

We believe that the actual special education services should be as close to the school community as possible. . . . The present operation is completely inconsistent with the new directions and in effect creates two school departments. The reassignment of 19 psychologists to the central office would almost certainly wipe out guidance services to the school, except for "tokenism." Placing them back under a senior psychologist would limit their role of service to the schools and the community and in effect relegate them to the former role of "testers" in the Research Department. This kind of a role change is philosophically opposed to current trends in the state and is particularly "suspect" in an area with large numbers of students from diverse racial and ethnic backgrounds. . . . The unification of pupil personnel services constitutes one of the most effective and far reaching aspects of decentralization to date. To do an about face and now centralize the major part of psychological services would destroy this unified support system and result in an expensive duplication of services.

The regionals also pointed out the existence of a recent precedent for their plan in the functions of the Office of Pupil Personnel Services. This unit had been partially decentralized with little dissension.

The director of special education issued a strong rebuttal in a memorandum to his superior, the associate superintendent for curriculum and instruction. He maintained, in part,

Oakland is not large enough, in my opinion, to decentralize special education; if it is properly done it will be excessively expensive because of the need for high quality special education administrators in each region with leadership at the central level to ensure continuity.

The trend in the nation is not in favor of decentralization of special education except in the largest cities where the programs have become tangled messes of bureaucracy.

This administrator then turned one of the regionals strongest arguments against them:

I believe also that the special education service should be as close to the community as possible. . . . Regions are not carbon copies of each other. Because of this, the need for centralization of special education is paramount. This cannot be left up to pupil personnel consultants who have other duties and have a primary responsibility for 90% of the regular children; hence, the 10% of the handicapped become a secondary function. In addition, the Pupil Personnel Consultants, in my opinion, either lack training, experience or understanding of the many ever changing special education facets in the areas of education codes, Title 5 regulations, evaluation procedures, fiscal problems . . . , etc. Since these are now adequately handled at the central level it appears imprudent to change for the sake of decentralization.

An equally damaging blow to the regionals' position is contained in the following comments, which speak directly to the general perception of the powerlessness of the three associate superintendents.

I would like to say that I have seen no difference between how we function centrally [and] how we now function regionally, as far as Special Education is concerned. . . . The impact from the Regions except for general principals meetings is nil. Where there is some question on matters of concern, things are unfortunately standing still.

In addition, this assessment should also be seen as a criticism of the superintendent. Decentralization was *his* plan and here was a subordinate who questioned the efficacy of the innovation. The implication was not discussed by the cabinet. Foster's mind was made up and that effectively forestalled further discussion. No one questioned the conceptual underpinnings of decentralization in Oakland; attention was devoted to resolving the immediate dispute between the director of special education and the regionals.

After studying the arguments Foster finally decided in favor of the director and centralization. In explaining the decision to the cabinet he maintained that it was based on the merits of the director's views. However, the director of special education had let it be known that he would resign, but not quietly, if his office were decentralized. This employee was in a strong position because of his national reputation in the field and his close ties with several members of the Board of Education. Had this threat been carried out, Foster believed that his administration, and thus his total plan for organizational change, would have been jeopardized. The relative weakness of the regionals and the decentralization of the system gave the superintendent few resources with which to fight for his associate superintendents, despite his basic agreement with their position. Moreover, Foster was in no position to press the issue so soon after his earlier setback from the board. And explaining decentralization in operational terms to the staff or members of the board was becoming increasingly difficult. Like the director of special education, these questioners could see few differences from the past. The regionals also felt the discomfort, for they found themselves in an exposed position with limited means to ward off their critics. Nor could the associate superintendents use their newly created positions. These were as yet untested and lacked legitimacy in the eyes of some of the staff and board members. And there was some resentment because the elementary schools had been ignored in filling the cabinet posts.

Superintendent Foster may have inadvertently contributed to the difficulties of his "alter egos" in his reply to a complaint that the three were all former secondary school principals. He told an elementary school principal:

in selecting them, the chief criteria were a full and solid grasp of the total educational challenge before Oakland, commitment and proven executive ability to move effectively within a large urban school enterprise. *I am depending on them, and holding them accountable, but not for their knowledge of secondary education, or their sympathetic understanding of the special needs of elementary schools.* We already have in our ninety schools the men and women who know best how to improve their programs. *It is not the job of the regional leader to second-guess our principals, or attempt to direct their efforts from the regional office.* ... The goal of decentralization is not to replace central office direction with regional office direction, it is the empowerment of each school to create and conduct its own successful enterprise. In this light, the role of Messrs. Reynolds, Carter and Croce is not to direct our secondary program with full confidence, and our elementary effort with perhaps less experience, but to cut free the constraints impinging on all schools, and deliver the resources principals say they must have. Theirs is not to direct, but enable; not to write prescriptions, but see that they are filled. [Emphasis added.]

It is possible to infer from the above that Foster failed to find the breadth of experience he wanted among the elementary principals. More important, however, Foster's letter was hardly likely to strengthen the regionals' efforts to carve out viable roles in the organization. The superintendent's statement also raises a question about his intentions for decentralization. If he in fact intended this plan to redistribute authority to the field, Baum's assessment of this issue bears repeating:

Ultimately, the problem of decentralization of authority becomes one of degree. There is no pure form or ideal type. We must judge decentralization by the extent to which individual units of an organization may select their own premises of action.[10]

The regionals were quite limited with regard to selecting premises for action. The superintendent's argument to the contrary notwithstanding, it is difficult to conclude that his decentralization program had a redistribution of authority as its principal purpose. Confusion about purposes may also arise because of a common assumption which equates decentralization with reductions in size. Frederick Terrien gave this issue careful attention in his research on decentralization at General Electric some years ago:

When an organization decentralizes, it does not dispose of or negate the inevitable process [of growth]; it merely adjusts to it in what appears to be a feasible manner. When an organization decentralizes . . . it must retain the same number of unit managers no matter where they are located. Indeed, it may have to add to staff by furnishing each of the managers with his own administrative component. . . . The growth of these subcomponents may, however, be held in partial check . . . by retaining most of the staff functions within the central . . . office.[11]

And had it not been for financial constraints and Foster's unwillingness to "empty" the central office, Oakland's decentralized regions would have looked much like the picture suggested by Terrien. The regional associate superintendents were each supposed to have a full administrative staff in addition to the principals of the more than ninety individual schools. (See Chart 5.) Terrien suggests, in addition, that some larger organizational purposes may be put "at risk" as a result of decentralization.

10. Baum, *Decentralization of Authority*, pp. 36-37.
11. Frederick W. Terrien. "Too Much Room at the Top?" *Social Forces* 37, no. 4 (May 1959): 304.

Chart 5. Oakland Unified School District
Proposed Organization Chart: A Decentralized Region

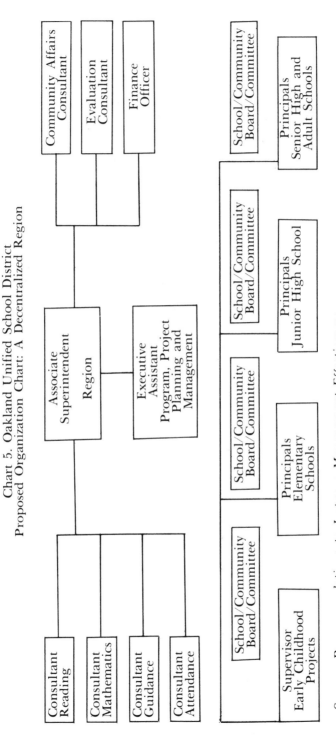

Source: *Recommendations to Improve Management Effectiveness*, Prepared for Marcus Foster, Superintendent of Schools, by Price Waterhouse and Co., San Francisco, California, 23 September 1970.

To a good many boards . . . executives and stockholders, decentralization may seem to violate the linkages of the company with a particular community, or to destroy the identity as a contained unit.[12]

However, since decentralization in Oakland did not disrupt existing school attendance boundaries, especially at the elementary level where the concept of neighborhood school is strongest, the risk of such violations was minimal. Foster seemed rather to believe

When the organizational structure is well conceived, . . . the process of identification permits the broad organizational arrangements to govern the decisions of the persons who participate in the structure.[13]

To be effective, however, these arrangement must be clearly understood by an organizational staff. Understanding implies communications and learning among the senior staff who establish the organization's structural arrangements and help to set its goals. It further requires that there then be effective means of information exchange between them and the staff responsible for goal implementation. Although the superintendent's cabinet was an efficient device for leadership communications, there was no counterpart for the school district's middle management, that is, the principals. Superintendent Foster instituted the practice of monthly luncheons with small groups of principals in an effort to meet this organizational need. He thus became a kind of management consultant to his middle management personnel. The educative function of leadership was reasonably satisfied by this device when the superintendent was discussing issues of community participation or decentralization. But, as we shall see in the following chapter, when the need to educate these staff in the technical requirements of PPBS arose it proved to be unsatisfactory.

DECENTRALIZATION: WHO BENEFITS?

From Foster's initial comments on the value of decentralization one would have expected an authority structure similar to that described by Norton Long:

12. Ibid.

13. Herbert A. Simon, *Administrative Behavior*, 2nd ed. (New York: The Free Press, 1957), p. 211.

A cooperating organization can operate successfully without a commanding hierarchy. Is this a special case of human behavior, or does it have implications for public administration? Science at least provides us with an example of organized human activity that solves problems without a formal directing hierarchy.[14]

In spite of the obvious weaknesses in his decentralization plan Foster continued, publicly, to treat it as a positive accomplishment. The regional offices were established without the full complement of staff recommended by Price-Waterhouse, which the superintendent knew was needed. This made it very difficult for the regions to deliver on Foster's promises. The regional associate superintendents told the superintendent and the others in the cabinet:

If we are to be held accountable for providing services to the school sites, and if we, as administrators, are going to be true to the promise of providing services to the local school site, then we must adequately staff the Regional Offices so that they may deliver the indicated services.

Instead of working on the implementation of decentralization much of their time was spent handling parents' complaints and attending meetings (including cabinet and board meetings). The teaching staff and others who had had their expectations raised had their own complaints. For them decentralization was little more than another layer of bureaucracy which made it even more difficult for teachers to secure needed services. To make matters worse, the problems with this first structural innovation were given broader circulation in a report prepared for the MPCC's Decentralization Task Force. This study specifically called attention to the paucity of resources given to the school site in saying: "There has been a subtle but pervasive emphasis in the decentralization on the regional level over the local school site."[15]

The report also strongly implied that the lack of resources at the local school was deliberately intended:

The Price-Waterhouse Study gives more emphasis to the establishment of regions, even listing it first in the conclusions. . . . Resources, though small, were allocated to establish the regional offices while no noticeable resources have gone to school sites.[16]

14. Norton E. Long, *The Polity* (Chicago: Rand McNally, 1962), p. 83.
15. The Decentralization Task Force of the Master Plan Citizens Committee, Oakland, California, *An Interim Evaluation of Decentralization in the Oakland Public Schools*, prepared by Knight, Gladieux & Smith, Inc., San Francisco, California, 26 July 1972, p. 21.
16. Ibid.

Even before this study was begun, the superintendent had anticipated its critical conclusions because of his commitment to innovate within "existing resource limits." Unfortunately others were not likely to give the same weight to this constraint. But Foster made no move to stop the MPCC; he decided to "take the heat."

While the results of the evaluation showed a number of intraorganizational problems which required attention, there were some positive findings. The regional associate superintendents were found to have spent considerable time on the community relations aspects of their new jobs. It is not surprising then that the community responded to decentralization in mildly positive terms. From their perspective, at least, a long-standing grievance about public education was finally being met. These positive feelings were also partly due to the creation of the MPCC as a structured vehicle for community participation.

The superintendent did not take the criticism in the report as a defeat. Indeed, when his staff returned for the opening of schools in the fall of 1972, he treated the report as a vindication of decentralization:

The whole process of decentralization has been looked at through the Master Plan by an independent . . . consulting firm. . . . [And] it's interesting to me as firm members talk with teachers, principals, citizens, that not one person is harking back to the old days. No one is saying that the concept is invalid. . . . [I]t's an interesting report to read, to see how, with limited resources, this process seems to be working and contributing something to the development of the school system.[17]

Thus, the principal beneficiaries of the changes instituted by Foster were the community and the superintendent himself. The community benefited because it now had a viable connection and a participative role in a major urban bureaucracy. And in Oakland much of the public seemed to recognize, as Herbert Kaufman has suggested, "Groups clamoring for local control of administrative programs . . . will probably discover that they get their most sympathetic hearings from chief executives."[18] The

17. Oakland Unified School District, *Superintendent's Bulletin* 53, no. 1 (September-October 1972): 6.
18. Herbert Kaufman, "Administrative Decentralization and Political Power," in *Public Administration in a Time of Turbulence*, ed. Dwight Waldo (Scranton, Pa.: Chandler, 1971), p. 12; see also Lowi, *At the Pleasure of the Mayor*, p. 207. A slightly different, but related example of an increase in executive power through decentralization is discussed by Dalton, Barnes and Zalesnik: "The Director . . . while the initiator of change, was also involved in

superintendent benefited from these changes by: (1) being perceived as responsive to legitimate community interests; (2) showing a willingness to extend himself personally to fulfill commitments to the public (he was responsible for getting the MPCC its own funds and ensuring that they were independent of the organization's control); (3) having the regionals intercept many of the small details which parents and community residents would otherwise bring to the "white house."

It is also important to recognize that even the limited public benefits described above provided the superintendent with a further political resource. Public support for his innovations reduced the likelihood of active internal resistance. But the damage to this part of Foster's organizational change was already done. The initiation of a significant departure in the structure of the system was made within "existing resource constraints." Even for those who heard this caveat, it meant little. The superintendent should have realized that he would still be expected to reduce those constraints somehow. His own and the cabinet's commitment to do the right thing were not enough. And conceptually the superintendent could not reconcile in his own thinking the need for him to give up power if the regionals were to be at all effective in their tasks. Of additional importance to the superintendent's plans was his failure to consider the prerogatives of others who would be involved in the implementation of change. For a man committed to sharing power and involvement it is ironic that his troubles with decentralization—his first systematic attempt at organizational change—should have resulted from inattention to the internal constituency. Moreover, the decentralization plan was the victim of the Price-Waterhouse team's arrogance or its ignorance of the informal organization in school systems.

---

redefining his power in the organization. At first glance it may appear as though he was relinquishing power through 'flattening' the organization of structure. Another interpretation of the effects of flattening leads to the conclusion that if anything his power increased through several effects. First, the new organization structure created a stronger bond between the Director and Junior Managers while weakening their bond with Senior Managers." Gene W. Dalton, Louis B. Barnes, and Abraham Zalesnik, *The Distribution of Authority in Formal Organizations* (Boston: Harvard University Division of Research, Harvard Business School, 1968), pp. 43-44.

They had not secured the ideas and concerns of the bureaucracy's middle management—the principals. And there was one more change to come, in which the principals were also expected to play a major role. In the following chapter we will examine the attempt to introduce a program budget in the Oakland public schools. As with decentralization this innovation was also initiated without widespread involvement. The program budget must be seen, however, as quite a different order of change than either decentralization or community involvement. A program budget imposes a knowledge burden which Oakland could not satisfy.

6

The Planning, Programming and Budgeting System and the Consolidation of Innovations

Following the lead of the federal government in the middle 1960s a number of smaller bureaucracies began to look at the program budget as a potentially powerful tool with which to attack their problem of resource allocation.[1] For Foster the planning, programming and budgeting system (hereafter referred to in abbreviated form as program budget, PPBS, or PPB) was an excellent vehicle for silencing the critics of public school systems for the latter's inefficiency. The program budget would also demonstrate Marcus Foster's awareness of the need for better managerial skills among educational administrators. The superintendent intended to show the board and Oakland's business community that he was a sophisticated manager, alert to recent developments in management and skillful in adopting them for the public schools. Foster

1. The literature on the PPBS concept is extensive. For those unacquainted with this literature a good starting point would be the special number of the *Public Administration Review* 26, no. 4 (December 1966), especially the articles by Allen Schick, "The Road to PPB: The Stages of Budget Reform," pp. 243-58, and Aaron Wildavsky, "The Political Economy of Efficiency," pp. 292-310. Little analysis of the federal retreat from PPB is available; however Allen Schick has developed a brief essay on the events leading to the 1971 memorandum signaling the end of the movement in his "A Death in the Bureaucracy: The Demise of Federal PPB," *Public Administration Review* 33 (March-April 1973): 146-56.

believed that the program budget would enable him to tie together his other changes. With this tripartite strategy—community involvement, decentralization and PPB—the Oakland public
schools could move in new directions leading to better pupil
performance. And it was Foster's commitment to attaining that
goal which formed the basis for each of the innovations he
attempted in Oakland.

As was the case with decentralization, the superintendent could
not give the board, or any other questioner, evidence that PPB
could do what he and Price-Waterhouse claimed. Even in the
federal government, where it had been most extensively adopted,
there was no conclusive evidence to show that the program budget technique worked. The board accepted Foster's claims for the
technique, however, because he took a strong position on this
innovation. And as with many outside government, Foster's understanding of this approach was limited. This weakness is explained by his less than systematic exposure to the conceptual
and technical foundations of PPB before coming to Oakland.

WHERE DID FOSTER GET THE IDEA
THAT PPB WOULD SAVE THE SCHOOLS?

Foster first learned about PPBS as a doctoral student in educational administration at the University of Pennsylvania. His
subsequent contact with this technique of management came
from the management firm of Price-Waterhouse, when they performed a management study for the Philadelphia schools. Led by
Philadelphia school superintendent Mark Shedd, the senior
members of the administration had participated in several brief
seminars at which PPB was described.

Blackburn had also been involved in this experience but he had
had some direct acquaintance with PPB as a Peace Corps director in Somalia during the Johnson administration. His experience was limited, however, since he had left the Peace Corps
shortly after the practice was adopted. Nevertheless, Blackburn
also believed that PPB "would help Oakland or any public
school system make sure that the money is where the district's
mouth is" in terms of educational policy and instructional programs. In his mind, PPB was a salvation. Indeed, few critics of
bureaucracy are prepared to argue against the notion that organizational leaders need to make better decisions. This is the point

made by Alice Rivlin in observing that PPBS is conceptually nothing more than common sense:

> Anyone . . . running a government program, or indeed any large organization, would want to take these steps to assure a good job: (1) Define the objectives of the organization as clearly as possible; (2) find out what the money was being spent for and what was being accomplished; (3) define alternative policies for the future and collect as much information as possible about what each would cost and what it would do; (4) set up a systematic procedure for bringing the relevant information together at the time the decisions were to be made.[2]

But common sense, as we know, is frequently an uncommon commodity. And as the Oakland public schools learned, taking the four steps outlined by Rivlin proved to be a formidable task. The common sense of the PPBS approach, its promise of rationality and better decisions, and its value as a symbol of change nevertheless all contributed to Foster's commitment to adopt it in Oakland. Finally, it is important to remember that the superintendent's belief in the potential of PPBS was strengthened by the arguments in its favor by the Price-Waterhouse firm, which had helped the Philadelphia schools begin the development of such a system in 1968.

CRITICISM WAS IRRELEVANT

As was the case with his other innovations, Foster did not seek the advice of others in the administration for this change in the organization's activities. He did not even fully discuss his ideas for PPB with Benbow—who had been business manager of the district for sixteen years, and was still retained as a financial affairs consultant—not so much because he didn't want Benbow's ideas as because he was already convinced that PPB was "doable."

As the former business manager, Dr. Benbow was the most knowledgeable critic of the attempt to institute PPB in Oakland. He believed it would be too costly in terms of hardware and additional personnel; moreover he was not persuaded that PPB would aid decisionmaking. Benbow also pointed out that he and the comptroller had studied PPB at length prior to Foster's arrival and had decided not to attempt its development. The costs

2. Alice M. Rivlin, *Systematic Thinking for Social Action* (Washington, D.C.: Brookings Institution, 1971), p. 3.

of the extremely detailed accounts and other record keeping integral to PPB reduced the concept's feasibility in his judgment. In addition Benbow could see no way of reconciling the political pressures which would result from community involvement and decentralization within a PPB framework. Nevertheless he did think the system had one redeeming feature: "Management by objectives is the best part of PPBS," Benbow said. There was, however, little that was new in this idea. Benbow observed that as business manager he and his division heads would "set objectives to be achieved, and periodically, every three months or so, . . . assess their programs and update the objectives." Despite the touted analytic sophistication implied in the program budget concept, Benbow was not persuaded of its suitability for the schools. Basically the former superintendent did not expect PPB to provide a more efficient way of managing the organization's budget.

Even if it had done so, he firmly believed that most of the public, especially parents, weren't nearly so interested in efficient use of their tax dollars as they were alleged to be. In his view the schools' public was primarily interested in whether or not "Johnny is learning." Dr. Benbow could see no way in which the program budget could help a student to learn or a teacher to teach. But the reservations of Spencer Benbow were ignored. He was, after all, an "old-line" business manager. Moreover he was due to retire in early 1971, and as a consultant without an institutional base there was little he could do about his beliefs.

Foster also had a powerful ally to assist him if he encountered any substantial opposition. The governor and state legislature were also concerned over the rising cost of public education. They shared Foster's view of the new management techniques as a way to impose controls upon expenditures in the public sector. By 1973 every school district in California was expected to change from the traditional line-item budgets to the program budget.

Some proponents of PPBS, such as Harry Hartley, argued that school systems would be able to benefit from the experience of others when they began to convert:

Schools will have the distinct advantage of being able to assess the performance of program budgeting in a number of kinds of organizations prior to adopting it.[3]

3. Harry J. Hartley, *Educational Planning-Programming-Budgeting: A Systems Approach* (Englewood Cliffs, N.J.: Prentice-Hall, 1968), p. 247.

There were few reasons for such optimism. Still, through September 1970, the Price-Waterhouse consultants were available to the superintendent and his staff to help resolve questions concerning PPB—if they had been asked. Once Price-Waterhouse completed its report, however, the district could not afford to give them another contract to assist in developing a program budget. And during the period when the consultants might have been used, the superintendent's attention was directed away from the issues implied in the conversion of the management processes of the schools, as Foster worked on his other innovations.

THE STATE WAS NO HELP

Nor was help forthcoming from other school districts around the state. They were, in many cases more uncertain about PPB than was Oakland. This was particularly true of the many small school systems in California. The state Department of Education tried to provide assistance through one-day county-wide seminars similar to those which Foster and Blackburn had attended in Philadelphia, but these seldom had much positive effect. These meetings were more concerned with the "phasing-in" problems of the state-wide mandate than with the technical and theoretical issues of PPBS.

According to the state's plan, phasing-in would proceed in the following fashion: planning for PPB during 1968-69; the fourteen pilot districts for PPB in the state to be selected during 1969-70; the advisory commission to conduct in-service training in these fourteen districts during 1970-71. In-service training on budgeting and accounting for PPB would be instituted during 1971-72, again in the pilot districts. Finally, implementation of PPB would take place in 1972-73 and the system would become operational during the 1973-74 school year. But no one knew whether that schedule could really be maintained. Nevertheless the state personnel expected a large number of school districts to become involved in PPB over and above the fourteen pilot districts, based on the principle of "each one teach one" from the experience gained at the in-service training sessions between 1970 and 1972.

Precious little was learned at these meetings. Individual school districts' representatives were usually outnumbered by those from the staffs of county superintendents in whose offices the seminars were generally held. And few budget officers were to be found among those attending, either from local districts or the county. To make matters worse, county superintendents' staffs were seldom of much assistance to their large urban school districts. The county offices were more commonly seen, and acted as, supplemental administration for small urban and rural school systems. Big-city school administrators were not in the habit of calling on the county staff. Instead they talked to their colleagues in other large California districts or those outside the state with whom they shared similar problems.

Added to these difficulties, over which the state had little control, was a problem of even greater consequence. At a meeting attended by Foster's deputy, for example, the state consultant admitted that the legislature's intent was to save money. Legislators knew that the people of California were unhappy at the alleged waste of tax dollars. The program budget, in the legislature's view, would constrain expenditures. In short, PPB would save money. That planning, programming and analysis might have broader implications within school systems was submerged by the desire of the state's political officials to "squeeze, trim and cut."

Unfortunately, the state officials were not sufficiently concerned that the expected efficiency deriving from PPB would cost money. And because most of the school systems didn't really understand what PPB was all about, the matter of its expense was seldom raised. Where were the funds to cover "start-up" costs to be found? State assistance was a possibility, it was believed, but these hints of help were put in the most general terms and in fact never materialized. Nor did the federal government rush in to fill the void.

Ignoring its lack of preparation, Oakland forged ahead with the development of a program budget. The new budget director and his key staff had to do extensive reading on their own to become even minimally acquainted with the new budgeting technique. At the same time, they were also getting ready to develop Foster's first budget submission to the Board of Education. And because the budget director was not experienced in the district's fiscal affairs (he had been in the ESEA programs office), he had to try to learn the old and the new while settling into his job.

REVENUE SOURCES CONSTRAIN PPB ·

Urban school districts, like many other urban bureaucracies, are fiscally dependent. Unlike the federal government or large private corporations (with whom they increasingly like to compare themselves), this group of public organizations has only a limited ability to generate the revenues which they require. The general purpose tax rate of the schools, for example, is established by a tax election and not by the governing board, and the Oakland public has been loathe to tax itself any more heavily to support the public schools. The state legislature had used this fact in turning down previous requests for funds. Revenue bonds can be issued, but there is a strong bias against indebtedness among members of the board. Moreover these bonds would still require voter approval. Finally, of course, school bond revenues can be used only for capital and plant improvements and not to support the general education program. Oakland, like most big-city school systems, needed general-purpose operating funds, not new buildings. And the opponents of construction bonds (at least in Oakland) are suspicious that construction may, in fact, be used as a subterfuge for new educational programming.

The program budget technique is of little help to budget makers who lack the flexibility to shift funds to meet internally determined needs. It is primarily useful in the allocation of resources which are discretionary, but the superintendent of schools in Oakland headed a system in which there was little such discretion. A substantial amount of his organization's revenues came from what are called "override" taxes, which could be imposed without voter approval. These taxes comprised more than one-third of the total local tax rate. But they have two strong strings attached. In some cases a maximum limit on the permissible levy is imposed by the legislature, and in all instances the override tax may be used only for a specific program. The impact of these constraints on budgetary behavior in Oakland becomes clear when we note that approximately 48 percent of the school district's tax revenue for 1972-73 was for restricted purposes only.[4]

Public school systems are also plagued by an added difficulty in regard to their budgeting practices. Many depend upon their

4. *Statistical and Financial Data: 1972-73*, Oakland Unified School District, p. 11. This figure represents an end point in a pattern of increasing use of such funds which began in the middle of the 1960s.

state legislatures for increments to their tax generated revenues. For Oakland, and for other California school districts, this frequently results in more than normal budgetary uncertainty. Budget development at the local level cannot be made to fit the budgetary politics of the state legislature. The adoption of the program budget technique by the Oakland public schools, or any other organization with similar troubles, would not, by itself, reduce this uncertainty.

PPBS THREATENS LOCAL CONTROL

In addition to their worries about where they would get the money to pay for the program budget, local schoolmen had another fear about what was likely to result from a statewide planning, programming and budgeting system. One member of the audience at the county seminar suggested that the state was about to dictate a state-wide system of education, thus destroying the tradition of local responsibility for public education. The state consultant agreed that a state-wide educational plan might indeed emerge from the development of PPB, but he minimized this prospect and went on to casually suggest that the districts themselves develop political muscle as a way to fend off any intrusion on local responsibilities. Some of the larger school districts, such as San Francisco, also expressed their concerns about the state's constraining effects on local fiscal flexibility. These constraints had to do with special override taxes, which only a handful of the smaller districts used in any case. Thus when one talked about the program budget in such meetings many of the participants heard different things. One came away from the seminar with the impression that efficiency potentials in PPBS had little impact. By March of 1971, however, Dr. Foster had decided that it was time to formally introduce his principals and other administrators to the concept of PPBS. A consultant was brought in to conduct two days of seminars at $500 a day. The results of these sessions were similar to those run by state consultants a few months earlier. There was only limited learning, but considerable confusion.

PPBS IN DECENTRALIZED ORGANIZATIONS

Because principals do not conceive of themselves as managers, they often regard anything resembling a money question as "central office stuff" to be avoided. While principals usually have had some training in educational administration, their administrative experience before principalship is generally limited. In most instances this experiential background of extensive dealing with children is not appropriate to the development of the management skills required to deal with a professional teaching and administrative staff. Nor, because of most teachers' classroom-bound orientation, does prior experience afford opportunities for the individual teacher to develop an integrated, organizational sense of his or her task. Thus a principal's grasp of the organization seldom includes more than his or her own school.[5] To some degree this view is a defense against the organization which

tends to operate as a never ending source of obstacles to those within the system, [so] that a major goal of the individual is to protect himself against the baleful influences of the system.[6]

And what is of especial importance to the introduction of change is the observation that *"this conception governs role performance even though* it may be a . . . faulty conception."[7]

One of the constants of a school system's organizational life which exacerbates the problem of role concepts among principals is their putative proprietary interest in their individual schools. To be sure, this "possession" may start as a semantic matter, but the longer a principal remains in a given school, the more do virtually all members of the organization accept the usage—"his school"—as though it were fact. What is more, the community of that school comes to identify the school site and a particular principal as one. All of these factors contribute to the difficulty of initiating change in public school systems.

5. Seymour Sarason has also made this point in an insightful study: "What I am suggesting is that being a teacher for a number of years may be in most instances antithetical to being an educational leader or vehicle for change. There is little in the nature of classroom teacher, there is little in the actual experience of the teacher with principals, and there is even less in the criteria by which a principal is chosen to expect that the role of the principal will be viewed as a vehicle, and in practice used, for educational change and innovation." *The Culture of the School and the Problem of Change* (Boston: Allyn and Bacon, 1972), p. 115. For a discussion of this problem in the Oakland schools, see my "A Policy Analysis of Resource Allocation in the Oakland Public Schools," unpublished, 1971, pp. 69-115.

6. Sarason, *Culture of the School,* p. 133.

7. Ibid., pp. 133-34. Emphasis in original.

One of the most outstanding organizational facts about school systems is the extent to which program responsibility may be centralized in the superintendent's office while implementation is decentralized to each of his principals. This fact alone would make it difficult to meet the criterion of comprehensiveness in the program budget. At the same time that Foster wanted the individual principals to respond to the needs of their immediate clientele, he was also insisting that this responsiveness remain consistent with district-wide priorities set by the central administration.

The effort to introduce PPB into the Oakland public schools highlighted an interesting feature about the organization of public school systems generally. These public organizations have a long history of site autonomy. That is, on most day-to-day matters, "urban schools display weak articulation between the individual school and the central office."[8] Indeed a principal's ability to exploit this weak articulation enhances his autonomy and frees him to develop projects for his specific school. Autonomy is also important in gaining a reputation as a good principal. Surely Foster must have known this, because he had capitalized on Gratz' autonomy in his rise to eminence in Philadelphia. The theoretical emphasis upon comprehensiveness and the superintendent's insistence that the principals think in terms of the district-wide goals and objectives was incompatible with "middle-management's" habits of thinking on a smaller scale.

Despite the organizational importance of principals, the Price-Waterhouse consultants chose to ignore them when they conducted the management survey. Why were they so cavalier in their handling of staff upon whom a superintendent must rely heavily for successful policy implementation? The management consultants sought out those with authority in the system. They believed the principals had none, as the following statement reveals:

Principals potentially have a great deal of discretion but right now they do not know how to use it. . . . We were interested in authority but it was

8. Morris Janowitz, *Institution Building in Urban Education* (New York: Russell Sage Foundation, 1969), p. 29. The issue of corrdination is also given explicit attention in Wildavsky, "The Political Economy of Efficiency," p. 304; see also Naomi Caiden and Aaron Wildavsky, *Planning and Budgeting in Poor Countries* (New York: Wiley, 1974), pp. 277-79.

clear from the outset that they [the principals] were told what to do, how to do it, and when.[9]

The principals' reactions were predictable, but unfortunate for organizational change in the Oakland public schools. The management report, when finally submitted, was greeted with little warmth. The principals believed that a variety of new duties were to be assigned them but that they would still be "second class" administrators with little influence in the decisionmaking process. This was especially the case since they had received no assurances that accountability would be complemented by control over allocations at the individual school. It was also unrealistic to expect the school principals to suddenly become planners. Planning in the context of PPB has been defined as

the process of deciding on objectives of the organization, on changes in these objectives, on the resources used to attain these objectives, and on the policies that are to govern the acquisition, use and disposition of these resources.[10]

Projecting a need for resources had always been the task of the business office, and the principals were content to leave it that way. For a principal the most critical question was the allocation of teachers to his individual school for the next year. This allocation was determined by a formula tied to his projected enrollment. How many teachers and of what kinds was determined by student demand for particular courses.

To plan is to decide, and to decide is to choose, all of which presupposes some degree of analysis by those responsible for the decisions. Principals do not analyze in terms of the total system. Nor until quite recently have other higher level school administrators done so. Principals have not done so because they rarely control any significant portion of their budgets, except perhaps for consumable items. And here their decisions did not require analysis. All they needed to do was apply allocation formulas based upon the number of professional staff in the school district. Planning and choice of the type that PPB demands implied a completely different role for the principals within the school system. The development of a new role conception among Fos-

9. This observation was made by one of the Price-Waterhouse officials who had participated in the management study.

10. Robert N. Anthony, *Planning and Control Systems: A Framework for Analysis* (Boston: Allyn and Bacon, 1965), pp. 16-18.

ter's "site-managers" could only come about through extensive retraining. The piecemeal approach of two-day seminars was clearly inadequate for this purpose. In fact, the Price-Waterhouse report had said as much. "We believe," the report stated, "that all principals, supervisors, consultants, coordinators, and directors will require management training on a continuing basis. This will encompass more than 200 positions."[11] Correcting the weakness would, it was estimated, have cost the district between $35,000 and $45,000. And that estimate was only for the first year of PPB. Foster simply did not have the money to pay for such a program. The superintendent was forced to admit that he was "laying it on the district pretty heavy." He and his deputy were concerned about the training needs of the principals, but not all of the cabinet members were sympathetic. One of the regional associate superintendents derisively remarked that the principals were looking for "cookbooks." If one had been available, Dr. Foster would gladly have given it to them. The proponents of PPBS had never said that their new management technique was inexpensive; indeed, they actually said little about costs of any kind. But there were sufficient warnings available to potential users if they had bothered to look. Several years before the Oakland schools began their experiment, the Chase Manhattan Bank had warned:

The fact that problems [with PPB] are cropping up should not be a surprise. Shortages of manpower and funds put limits on progress. Changing from one system to another inevitably causes bottlenecks. And there is a more fundamental problem: moving from theory to fact opens up a host of pragmatic questions.[12]

A respected student of educational administration had specifically called attention to the pragmatic questions for public school systems considering the program budget:

[It] would require substantial increases in accounting staff, . . . developing a separate department of budget planning and system analysis and appraisal.[13]

11. *Recommendations To Improve Management Effectiveness*, Prepared for Marcus Foster, Superintendent of Schools, Oakland Unified School District, Price, Waterhouse and Co., September 1970, p. 26.

12. *"The Planning-Programming-Bugeting System,"* in *Business in Brief* (New York: Chase Manhattan Bank, December 1967), pp. 3-4, quoted in Harry J. Hartley, *Educational Planning-Programming-Budgeting*, pp. 126-27.

13. H. Thomas James, "Modernizing State and Local Financing of Education," in *A Financial Program for Today's Schools* (Washington, D.C.: Committee on Educational Finance, National Education Association, 1964), p. 59.

The Price-Waterhouse study had prepared Foster for the increased needs pointed out by James in the passage just cited. However, that report had given him little guidance on the place of analysis in PPBS. As a result the Oakland public schools engaged in little appraisal of past or current activities in preparation for adopting district-wide goals and objectives. Instead planning function was implicitly accepted as a part of the ongoing responsibilities of the superintendent's cabinet. The leadership core did what it could to think about the future, but in general the future was relegated to a subordinate position by the press of routine matters.

Foster tried to cut down on the use of cabinet meetings by attempting to see his associate superintendents by appointment during the week. The effort was short-lived, however, because it reduced his ability to maintain frequent contacts with outside groups. And to a lesser degree the regional associate superintendents had a similar problem. For consistent with Foster's view that they act as his alter egos, the regionals were trying to emulate the superintendent in dealing with their public.

To analyze policy an organization must know where it wants to go. But calling for the development of objectives and goals by everyone, the superintendent appeared to be asking for direction. He told his staff and the public, however, of his intention to

submit to the Board by Oct. 13 meeting a draft . . . of the overall goals of the Oakland Unified School District. . . . These "departure goals" will have been developed out of my experience with urban education, out of the experience of senior staff members, out of the conversations I have had around the city with a variety of groups, from points made in our special study [the Price-Waterhouse report] and from documents that show what this system is doing performance-wise for children. In other words, the goals will not be picked out of thin air.[14]

The above statement implies that some amount of analysis had been conducted as the basis for the "departure goals." But Foster was drawing on his own experience, the Price-Waterhouse study and standardized test results to discover what Oakland was doing "performance-wise." The Price-Waterhouse study had been primarily concerned with management activities and was not to any significant extent a careful analysis of educational processes in

14. Foster, *Making Schools Work* (Philadelphia: The Westminster Press, 1971) p. 160. Emphasis in original.

the Oakland schools. The district had a wealth of test results for Oakland's students and considerable amounts of socioeconomic data, but the school system lacked the ability to carry out basic research. Thus the research office could not provide much in the way of evaluation to assist in analysis. Moreover, the combined experience of the superintendent and his senior staff did little more than confirm what they already knew. The district's non-white students were not faring well.

Perhaps an intensive analytical effort would have made a difference. In lieu of specific analyses of education in Oakland, however, the superintendent called for members of the organization to begin developing objectives. "Each teacher should take on the heavy personal and professional responsibility for setting his own instructional objectives for this year. . . . It should be possible to define what you want to do in terms of measurable units."[15] As an alternative to fashioning a program structure, this fragmented development of objectives obviously left something to be desired. It is difficult to see how this set of activities could help the school district meet Carlson's recommendation, "to make possible better analysis of [individual school] programs by organizing cost and output information so as to include all areas relevant to a problem."[16] Dr. Foster, in any case, appeared to have another objective in mind. It was the output side of the issue which concerned him. The superintendent's message was, in fact, a call for the teaching staff to develop performance objectives. And these measures were not to be used solely to measure individual performances:

Each school shall state its objectives, in similar terms, for the year, with a target date for a brief working statement by November 15. As each classroom teacher outlines what he is planning to do for his children, these objectives collectively become the objectives of the entire school. Even as we establish long-range and difficult goals that make us reach beyond what we are now, we should choose objectives that we can use as indicators of progress.[17]

15. Ibid., p. 163.
16. Jack W. Carlson, "The Status and Next Steps for Planning, Programming and Budgeting," in *Public Expenditures and Policy Analysis*, ed. Robert H. Haveman and Julius Margolis (Chicago: Markham, 1970), p. 371.
17. Ibid., p. 164.

But Oakland's teachers objected to the superintendent's request that they prepare measurable objectives. The same kinds of objections were raised among various agencies of the federal government in response to the need to measure performance. As John Capozzola has pointed out, "Measuring organizational performance quantitatively irritates those who are value-oriented, emotionally oriented, politically oriented, or just do not understand."[18]

MEASURABLE OBJECTIVES
AND THE RELUCTANCE TO QUANTIFY

By a coincidence of bad timing, Foster's call for performance objectives came at a time when the legislature was considering a bill to require annual evaluations of teacher performance. The teachers' organizations saw these moves as calculated attempts to erode their job security. In addition, the superintendent's professional colleagues had reservations.

Dr. William Carey, the superintendent of a small, upper-income California school district admitted the need for performance objectives but also noted:

[If] our wisest educational decisions are based on the objectives which we can produce, we risk distorting our task. . . . The widespread commitment to the production of performance objectives assumes that we are already convinced that the use of our resources for the production of such objectives will produce an improved educational program. But this conclusion is at best tentative, if not totally unwarranted. The state of the teaching art is such that we are able to produce only the most primitive performance objectives at this time. They will be . . . constructed in accordance with rigid definitional requirements; consequently our objectives will be ritualistic, artificial and stylized. . . . The writing of performance of objectives dealing with the affective consequence of instruction will most likely be ignored since the more difficult an objective is to write, the less likely it is to be written at all.[19]

And there was an even more dire consequence to come; because these objectives were so expensive to produce, Carey believed,

18. John M. Capozzola, "PPBS: Systemization or Revolution in Government Management," *Governmental Research Association Reporter* 18, no. 1 (First Quarter, 1966): 4, quoted in Harry J. Hartley, *Educational Planning-Programming-Budgeting*, p. 231.

19. William Carey, "Mismanagement by Objectives," *California Journal for Instructional Improvement* 13 (March 1970): pp. 18-19.

they would become institutionalized, thus reducing the "possibility for modification and refinement by the day-to-day practitioner."[20]

Again, however, the doubts and reservations of outsiders were not treated as applicable to Oakland's case. Foster's deputy commented that management by objectives was only a "teacher's lesson plan writ large—it's projected over a year rather than one day." The superintendent saw management by objectives as the only way to "make a track record." In asking his teachers and principals to set objectives for themselves, Foster believed he was only asking them to raise their levels of aspiration for the students. The teaching staff heard him asking for something quite different. That interpretation was consistent with what J. D. Frank had defined as an aspiration level: "The level of future performance in a familiar task, which an individual, knowing his level of past performance in that task, explicitly undertakes to reach."[21] Overall, the objectives stated by the teaching staff were conservative because they didn't want to take the risks entailed in stating more optimistic objectives.

PPBS MEANS DIFFERENT THINGS
TO DIFFERENT PEOPLE

The program budget came to be regarded as many things before it had become anything. The regional associate superintendents seized on the planning aspect of the concept, but what they called planning meant little more than time to meet with their limited personal staffs to "noodle." Systematic examination of goals and objectives, assessing resource needs and the mapping of alternative strategies for goal achievement were not the concerns of the regionals, who considered them problems for the "white house" staff. When the regionals thought about PPB—which was seldom—they all seemed to agree that it was dehumanizing, in its emphasis on "numbers and not people." One associate superintendent contended that in making budget allocations through programs the district would lose the sensitivity to human problems and needs which is vital to an effectively functioning school system. To underline this point he stated, "I hope that PPB will

20. Ibid., p. 19.
21. J. D. Frank, "Individual Differences in Certain Aspects of the Level of Aspiration," *American Journal of Psychology* 47 (1935): 119.

be more than just telling me it costs $5.26 to teach that kid to draw a straight line!" But he and his colleagues were uncertain that the system would be able to do more than just that.

Even the associate superintendents in the central office found themselves pressed for time to adequately deal with the problems of PPB. The associate superintendent for planning, research and evaluation frankly stated that he had "damn little time to look ahead—I need time to look at the next steps in PPB." To some extent, however, he believed that the school budget had a built-in planning function, but only because in his view planning was connected with the use of the school plant and land purchases. When he did think of the planning needs in PPB, it was in narrow fiscal terms. He maintained that "formal [planning] means fiscal planning, that is, anticipating the size of next year's possible deficit, the size of the next annual tax base, and the state of legislation which might affect the state's allocation to the schools." After attending to these immediate matters and the other tasks assigned him by the superintendent, he could think about PPB in "what little bits [of time] we can squeeze out." He would undoubtedly have agreed with his colleague in the field who bluntly stated, "There simply is not enough time for long-range planning, taking a long and relaxed look at the needs of the region. We're on a kind of day-by-day existence!" Nor was there much disagreement with this view across regions. Another of the regionals ruefully admitted, "We'd almost have to be able to walk on water and leap high mountains" to do what was promised when they first took office. Even the deputy superintendent somewhat jokingly suggested that PPBS was "Kafkaesque" in its consequences.

At the same time the associate superintendent for management systems, who had the primary responsibility of establishing the PPBS accounts, emphasized the notions of accountability and control as potential benefits from adopting this concept of management. He believed that part of the difficulty in establishing PPB in the Oakland public schools was that there had been no control function with regard to the expenditure of funds. There were no means under the old budgetary process to tell how rapidly funds were being expended. As a result the individual schools spent their allocations much too rapidly, and did not know until late in the school year that they had exhausted their funds. He complained also that the data processing system was not used to develop an "audit trail" for expenditures by district staff, but rather was simply called upon to report the amount of expenditures.

If PPB were successfully developed and implemented it would force individual unit managers (central office directors) and site managers to be accountable for the activities of their individual units or sites. The head of management systems believed that most of the field staff regarded the central office staff as "holding the club" which got things done. He tried to persuade the principals, however, that the accountability aspect of PPB would naturally give control of the "club" to the local school site once decentralization took hold. This was "a way to get people to police their own actions," he said, "or to become their own auditors." Perhaps a more meaningful consequence of putting this kind of accountability at the local site is the following: there would be no way under PPBS for the principal to pass the buck for something that was not done or was done poorly.

The head of management systems agreed with the superintendent on the capability of PPB to monitor through the evaluation of goal achievement or failure. In his view it was the monitoring and evaluation aspect of PPB which gave the superintendent the most grief, because the teachers disliked the idea that they should be monitored at the end of each year based on goal statements made earlier in the school year.

Despite such opposition, however, this associate superintendent insisted that "if monitoring and evaluation is not carried out, there really is very little argument to be made for PPB." The new management technique could be used to make better resource allocation decisions, but not as a means to cut costs; "efficiency is not necessarily a part of PPBS," he stated.

Thus a program budget was expected to allow the central office administration to fix responsibility for performance, good or bad. The principal would have control and accountability for the allocation of resources to meet site objectives as he, his staff, and the local community collectively determined them. Early on all members of the cabinet held this view of a rationalistic organizational future. PPB may indeed suggest a means to redistribute power to "accountable unit managers," as Price-Waterhouse had stated, but when power is hedged about by resource constraints and the requirement that it be shared with others in unaccustomed ways, there is no reason to expect anything other than confusion and uncertainty. Still, none of the superintendent's key men would ask the hard question: was a program budget feasible and useful for Oakland?

THE BOARD WAS CONFUSED

Considering the knotty problems already recounted, Foster was fortunate that the Board of Education was not overtly hostile to PPBS. In discussing some of the problems of PPB at the federal level, Fred S. Hoffman has noted the existence of three types of difficulties between the executive and the legislature:

> They are characterized under three headings: lack of PPB output, lack of congressional access to the existing PPB output, and lack of interest in (or actual antipathy) in some quarters of Congress to the things that PPB is striving to do.

But the Oakland schools' governing body was simply confused. For them PPBS was "the biggest mystery in the city," as one long-time school director phrased it. This confusion was related to the first of Hoffman's difficulties. A year and a half after Foster had to "go to the mat" to get the board to approve the purchase of a new computer system for PPBS the board was still looking for some product. After all the new system had cost Oakland $750,000 and they wanted to see something. Pity the head of the newly created management systems office, who tried to get his colleagues and the board to understand the problems involved in trying to develop what he estimated would be almost 35,000 accounts.[22] In addition he was embarrassed by the tremendous costs of his operation—over $14,000 a month for two data processing systems.

In anticipation of some hard questions the head of management systems prepared a response for the superintendent. The accomplishments which Foster could cite in justifying the expen-

---

22. A little careful reading of scholarly literature would have revealed the following observation from Herbert Simon: "The first step toward a performance budget involves a major reclassification of . . . accounts so that we can discover how many dollars are being spent to provide each service." Herbert A. Simon, "Staff and Management Control," *The Annals of the American Academy of Political and Social Science* 292 (March 1954): 98.

diture were hardly what one would expect from a program budget. The head of management systems wrote:

The accomplishments have been significant. 27,000 secondary students are now on our master file and those files have been used to implement scheduling for this fall. We have created Notices of Employment for 14,000 employees and have completed successfully the first round of payrolls using the system. The second round will be producing [sic] and distributing this Friday and represents in excess of 8,000 pay checks. The cooperation throughout the district has been magnificent from the local school site in submitting the data, to the changed system required in the payroll office, to the creation of a central records office and to the round the clock efforts of the data processing office personnel.

This statement might have led the board to recall an exchange with the former business manager three years earlier. A board member had

raised a general question about the use of electronic data processing equipment. He wondered if the equipment [were] actually saving money for the district and if the district [was] using its computers enough. . . . "Several companies which have employed electronic equipment extensively have determined that in the long run . . . there really are not enough savings to justify their expense." "We're in line with what other . . . districts are doing," said the business manager. "They could be wrong too," replied the board member.[23]

Although many members of the public wanted the schools to be more efficient—that is, reduce costs—there was no easy way for them to know, except when they received their annual tax bills, whether Foster's administration could meet this goal.

The superintendent tried to show that the organization was being more efficient when they reassigned personnel to the regions and when some staff was redeployed to make up the task forces to meet ad hoc internal needs. The presumed rationality of an economic firm, however, was more elusive, and paradoxically the method by which Foster sought to achieve it was costly.

In an effort to mute some of the criticism which might be expected to follow from the decision to implement PPB, especially since there were no immediate benefits in sight, the superintendent acted on a further recommendation from the consultant firm. For about three months several staff members from the budget office did double duty recasting the budget in program

23. *The Montclarion,* 9 April 1969.

terms while also preparing the standard line-item budget to meet state requirements. It was a good public relations stroke, and most of those who viewed the program document agreed that it was easier to study and understand than in the past. But this was also costly in staff time, and duplicating costs (the program budget was almost 600 pages long whereas the traditional budget was seldom more than 75 pages). And with the requirement to furnish copies to the public for their scrutiny these latter costs could be considerable.

Nevertheless some of the board members did expect that the introduction of PPBS would help the district to decrease the number of man-hours needed for attending to administrative detail. And still others expected that it would save the district some money relative to the decentralization of certain functions. What these functions might be the board members could not say. Generally most board members held a "hope it doesn't fail" attitude.

PPBS AND BUREAUCRATIC POLITICS

Despite Foster's oft-stated desire to shift power and resources to the field, this goal was not achieved. Prior to Foster's arrival the superintendent had not been a major actor in the budgetary process; it was an area left largely to the business manager. In Oakland, as in many other school districts, business managers were often more influential than the superintendent. The former business manager stated that he had "followed a guy who had practically been the superintendent of schools." A graphic illustration of this particular business manager's prestige was the fact that the board's executive sessions were held in his conference room and not that of the superintendent. Foster very quickly stopped this practice when he took over. He became the focal point for his organization's activities. His changes had put the system in a state of flux until such time as they became fully institutionalized. From the perspective of the board members the ability to secure reliable information through informal channels was inhibited by the need for adjustment entailed by Foster's moves.

PPBS is a technical process and those whom Foster had to convince—especially the staff from the former business office— could match their expertise against that of the superintendent. In financial matters the superintendent was on "their" turf and he was a novice. Had the superintendent been able to secure the board's full confidence in PPB and his own budgetary expertise, he might have encountered fewer difficulties with this sophisticated technique. But the Board of Education had known when they hired him that Foster lacked experience with school budgets. Moreover, after Foster had fashioned his "leadership core," he still had no one to whom the Board of Education would give its trust on budgetary and fiscal matters. The inability to gain the board's trust was also exacerbated by a conflict between the organization's comptroller, the new head of the management systems division and the budget office. As mentioned earlier, the comptroller was an old employee of the schools and, with the former business manager, was critical of the feasibility of PPB for the Oakland schools. Management systems and the budget office had a clear division of labor in that the former division was to provide a set of support services to the budget office staff, but it could not do so without also gaining some degree of control of the system's accounting practices. And the district's accounting was the province of the comptroller.

The system of accounts used by Oakland had been established in accordance with state procedures based upon the traditional practices associated with the line-item budget. Thus the movement toward PPB was stalled by the separation of budgeting from accounting. The general problem with this separation was essentially that the comptroller often has a pre-audit power to disallow expenditures. At the federal level Herbert Simon has noted that this power led to

a system of dual authority over expenditure . . . that has generally received adverse comment from persons who have studied it. It should be recognized, however, that this is merely an extreme form of the problem that arises whenever control functions of *any* sort are vested in an accounting unit. To the extent that the [comptroller] has authority to set limits to the actions of executives in the line organization, his authority cuts across the regular lines of authority, and the unity of command in the broad sense . . . is violated.[24]

Under the earlier practices of the school district this separation of functions had not presented any difficulties. Obviously this was in part a result of the close personal relations between the

24. Simon, "Staff and Management Controls," p. 168.

business manager and the comptroller. But the comptroller had been passed over for the new job of associate superintendent for management systems and Foster's new management concept contained a threat to his status in the organization.

The associate superintendent for management systems was unable to persuade his key staff that PPB was in fact the way in which Oakland could best achieve the goals of sound administration. Failing to persuade, he could have exercised his power to dismiss these staff members, but to do so would entail other, more costly, political risks. The superintendent did not want to draw additional attention to his problems with PPB. Dismissal of recalcitrant staff, especially those with good board relations, would have required a substantial use of his resources. Since he had heavily invested these resources to get board approval of PPB he wasn't sure that he could afford a victory which was likely to result in the enmity of at least three of his board members. Foster and his associate superintendent decided to "live with it." They hoped that eventually the comptroller would come around or that he might voluntarily leave the organization, since it was clear that he had no opportunities for advancement in Oakland as long as Foster was superintendent of schools.

THE "OVERHEAD COSTS"
OF PPB FOR LEADERSHIP

The adoption of PPB imposes additional costs which are seldom noticed. One of these is the erosion of a leader's time, perhaps his most limited resource. Implementation of this complex information processing system requires considerable coordination and planning of joint activity. Coordination of this sort is most effectively produced only by command, but to make sure that commands are followed the leaders must be directly involved. And for PPB, says Hoffman,

The interest and attention of the head of each department or agency or of his deputy are crucial to the success of PPB. The prototype of PPB was created by Secretary McNamara who considered the job of managing the resources of the Defense Department as among his prime responsibilities.[25]

25. Fred S. Hoffman, "Public Expenditure Analysis and the Institutions of the Executive Branch," in *Public Expenditures and Policy Analysis*, ed. Robert H. Haveman and Julius Margolis (Chicago: Markham, 1970), p. 441.

This should not be taken to mean that Foster, as the chief executive, could stand apart from what was happening to PPBS even though his preferred style was "to get out of the way" and let his staff take over once a policy was operational. The danger in this, which the superintendent recognized, is that the leader "can get too far away. . . . If you're not there it loses your thrust." With regard to the adoption of PPB Foster and others would do well to consider the comments of the former assistant director of the Bureau of the Budget:

> although the president expects his cabinet officers and their immediate subordinates to assist him in many capacities, he must accord high priority to the role of resource manager if . . . resources are to be used more efficiently.[26]

What has been detailed in the foregoing pages is an account of how a strongly held policy view can preclude critical questioning. It is also the case that a desire for change can become contagious to the extent that those upon whom a political executive depends for help get caught up in the spirit of creating something "different." The effect is the same. Questions are not asked, implications are not considered, alternatives are not discussed. And when there is help available from outside sources, it is ignored. (This should not be taken to mean that all outside help is worthwhile, for it demonstrably is not.) The case of PPB in Oakland also shows that collective ignorance can play an influential part in the failure of hard questions to emerge in the policymaking process. This is especially difficult to overcome in an area where the leader has expressed strong personal preferences.[27]

26. Ibid., p. 440.
27. Cf. Irving L. Janis, *Victims of Group Think* (Boston: Houghton Mifflin, 1972), chapter 1 and pp. 196-202.

7

Leadership: Change, Control and Achievement

Marcus Foster did not treat his plans for changing the Oakland public schools as ends in themselves. The three innovations were expected to produce two benefits: first, Foster anticipated an increase in the educational performance of Oakland's students, and second, these same innovations would create a new organizational form for urban school systems. In developing his plans for change the new superintendent addressed himself to three of the most vigorously expressed criticisms of public bureaucracy. Critics who seized on the assumed insularity of bureaucracy were the immediate audience for Foster's plans for community involvement and participation. A more restricted audience which faulted the hierarchical distribution of authority in formal organizations found Foster to be in sympathy with their position. Because he did share some of their outlook, the superintendent planned to decentralize power in the organization. The third innovation which Foster wanted for his organization was expected to demonstrate that public bureaucracies could become as efficient in the use of resources as many asserted was the case with private firms. Efficiency and rationality were the twin objectives of his attempts to develop and adopt the program budget.

Foster did not begin the introduction of change with the tentativeness of the novice. He moved quickly to give tangible meaning to his plan for community involvement when he gave the community a voice in the selection of principals. This was elaborated through the creation of the Master Plan Citizens Committee. Moreover, Foster's successful efforts to secure funds for the MPCC was clear evidence of the seriousness of his intentions with regard to participatory decision making in the Oakland schools. Foster, like many other advocates of participatory democracy, expected involvement to result in a more cooperative relationship between the organization and its public. Such cooperation, he believed, could also be converted into support for revenue measures which the school system needed. The emphasis given to community involvement also reflected the belief of education professionals that such involvement leads to improved educational performance by students. In view of Oakland's difficulties in this latter area it is not surprising that the superintendent's second innovation, decentralization, was also partially addressed to enhancing the community role. Community involvement received the greatest amount of Foster's attention. Frequent public engagements and accessibility to various individuals and groups contributed to the success of this innovation. But from the standpoint of organizational leadership this was, perhaps, the easiest change to accomplish.

Foster's strong belief in the merits of participation was quickly accommodated by a permissive environment for this type of change. It is also important to recognize that the superintendent did not require the resources of other members of his organization to make participation work. It was unnecessary because Foster was not directly changing the organization. Community involvement was directed outside and, initially, it did not affect the normal routines of the system's staff. Where Foster did seek help, as with securing foundation support for the MPCC, he knew what kind he needed. Moreover he knew where such aid was likely to be available and, once it was given, how it was to be employed. Again, however, the superintendent controlled the necessary resources to make this innovation a success.

Nor was community involvement the radical change that some may have expected. Foster's plan was an elaboration of the traditional community role in local education. It was innovative, however, because he expanded the kinds of roles which citizens might fill, and provided a systematic means for exchanging information and views between the school system and a public considerably enlarged by the involvement of non-whites. It was the meaning which Foster gave to community involvement that represented a significant change. The creation of the MPCC was his crucial first step toward achieving an ecological relationship between the public bureaucracy he led and its social and political environment. Perhaps because of the ease with which the system had adapted to community participation Foster did not expect serious problems with the move toward decentralization. However, decentralization was a different order of change. With this innovation the superintendent began to alter his organization directly. Much of the rationale for this innovation stressed the degree to which it would contribute to the full development of meaningful community involvement.

But Foster also insisted that decentralization would make the preparation of the program budget an easier task. This view stemmed from a belief that decentralized goals and objectives, developed by community residents and school staff, would logically become part of the program structure in the new approach to budgeting. The superintendent characterized this innovation as "empowering the local school site," meaning that he wanted those most closely connected with the educational problems in each region to develop individualized plans. But it is one thing for a group of individuals to develop goals and objectives, and something completely different for the group to carry them out. The former requires little power to execute, but the latter rests on the possession of resources and the ability to use them.

The plan to decentralize the Oakland public schools foundered on two issues. One of these, which Foster acknowledged, was the need to introduce this change within existing revenue constraints. The other, which was unexpected, was the necessity of reducing someone's power in order to redistribute it to the regions. Both of these issues were contained in the dispute between the regionals and the director of psychological services. The director was unwilling to give up his power in the organization. And he possessed sufficient strength to resist the effort by the regionals. If Foster had sided with the regionals he would have had to exercise precisely that kind of unilateral action which decentralization was said to make unnecessary. Since there was little slack in organizational resources, the superintendent could do little to make the regionals' positions more credible.

Foster was willing to accept the form of decentralization without the substance, in part because he placed a high value on organizational stability. Moving quickly to give the regionals power would, in addition, have forced him to violate one of his own beliefs about leadership. That is, he would not resort to the use of his executive power to order the decentralization because it would have damaged the image of cooperative leadership which he was trying to create. In any event Foster accepted the fact that for a time effective decision making for the schools would continue to be centralized. He continued to believe, however, that when the revenue situation eased decentralization could be made an effective part of the organization.

Decentralization did produce a benefit for the schools and the superintendent. And, paradoxically, it was partially a result of minimizing disruption. The regional plan effectively preempted an area of potentially serious conflict. Due to the racial makeup of the student body and school enrollments, questions of de facto segregation might have been expected in Oakland. But the carefully devised plan for achieving socioeconomic and racial balance in the newly created attendance areas reduced the likelihood of public controversy on this issue. As with community involvement, a good part of this achievement resulted from Foster's ability to control the development of the regional plan. The superintendent had very clearly specified what he wanted, and getting it depended little on the resources of others in the organization.

The third of Foster's innovations, the program budget, was expected to rationalize decision making. Based upon the goals and objectives that were expected to come from decentralization, the cabinet would be in a position to make the "best" decision in allocating resources to various organizational tasks. This would have produced a twofold benefit. Budgetary decisions would become more objective in the sense that the superintendent and his cabinet would presumably know if a particular decision was consistent with the agreed-upon objectives and the schedule of priorities. And the program structure of the new budget document would be much more understandable for the Board of Education and public during budget hearings.

This attempted innovation encountered troubles from the start. New computer facilities were required, putting added strain on an already limited financial situation. Technical assistance from the state was not forthcoming. Program accounts for PPBS were not compatible with state accounting requirements based upon a line-item budget and the conversion process was time-consuming and costly. Assuming that these difficulties could have been resolved (a heroic assumption at best), the program budget posed a unique problem. Here was an innovation for which Foster could draw on no prior experience. There were no instances of success with full PPBS to which the superintendent and his staff could look for guidance. Foster's commitment to this change was based on his belief that it could be accomplished. Although they acknowledged a need for technical aid, neither Foster nor his key staff knew what kind to seek or where it might be found. The superintendent's belief that the program budget could be developed overwhelmed any impulse by the members of his cabinet to raise questions. The more questions were not asked, the more the superintendent's commitment became a group phenomenon, further diminishing the likelihood of questions.

A decisionmaking style, which encouraged healthy skepticism, might have increased the chances for a careful examination of the suitability of PPBS for the Oakland schools. A search for answers to the hard intellectual and technical questions inherent in the concept of a program budget might have given Foster pause. Ironically, the problems with the program budget were attributable to the fact that Foster did control the innovation effort. It was the power of his own belief which dominated that of other members of the cabinet. And it was his control of the cabinet which effectively inhibited an examination of this innovation.

Still, the effort was not a complete failure. The Oakland schools did begin to look more carefully at their budgetary practices. The school administrators had taken the first tentative steps toward a more systematic appraisal of education and the kinds of activities that offered some prospect for improving student performance.

After three years of trying to change the Oakland public schools Marcus Foster was forced to admit that his hopes had not been completely realized. True, he could take credit for improved relations between his organization and the community. But the superintendent took little comfort in this accomplishment. Indeed, Foster voiced his disappointment over the lack of progress with decentralization and the program budget early in 1972. At that time the associate superintendents were still complaining about their lack of sufficient staff. The head of Planning, Research and Evaluation attempted to argue that he could save the district money if only he had more people. Dr. Foster unhesitatingly told him. "When you're failing it [is] difficult to persuade critics that you need more staff." For Foster it simply was not enough to have created a supportive constituency.

There was also some bitterness. In a speech before the American Association of School Administrators, the superintendent of schools charged:

[B]lacks become superintendents only in cities like mine, where the percentage of non-whites has reached 78 percent. Black educators don't get called into "cushy" jobs, schools, either. We go through a coronary alley at all those tough high schools and they tell us, "Here it is baby, make it fly!" Then when you can't make it, they say, "I told you those niggers can't do it!"[1]

This was not the first time that he expressed this sentiment, but it was the only time he had done so publicly. Still, Foster was expressing a view which other black administrators shared with him. Like him, these individuals had private resentments about the public's expectations of rapid solutions to problems of long standing. Although Oakland showed little visible response to Dr. Foster's remarks, he sent a more moderate letter on the school system and his tenure to the *Oakland Tribune* two weeks later. He emphasized the achievements of the school system under his leadership. Despite the acknowledged lack of definitive success with all of his changes, the superintendent derived satisfaction from setting them in motion.[2] Nonetheless, Foster knew that he had made promises to the Board of Education and to the public. His audiences were a bit restive over the seeming lack of improvement in the students' academic performance. The gains in reading scores which the school staff reported from time to time were unsatisfactory when measured against the expectations which the

1. *Oakland Tribune*, 21 March 1973, p. f-13; see also the *San Francisco Chronicle*, 21 March 1973, p. 4. The figure of 78 percent used by Foster refers to the student population, not the city's total.

2. James Payne employs the idea of "program incentive" in an effort to explain this satisfaction from working on one's policies. See the discussion in James L. Payne, *Incentive Theory and Political Process* (Lexington, Mass.: D. C. Heath, 1972), p. 84.

superintendent had helped to create. Even here, however, Foster could gain some satisfaction. His critics were less hostile than he might have expected them to be. And they were not expressing opposition to what he was trying to do. That is, organizational changes were evaluated independently of student achievement. This comes as no real surprise when we consider that most of the innovations were taking place inside the organization. There was little for the public to see. But there were some things which were readily apparent.

Student vandalism had not decreased and it was easy for citizens to see the evidence in the broken windows of school buildings. Violence in the school district seemed to be on the rise. The combination of violence, a new problem, and limited academic improvement, a persistent old problem, forced Foster to give less time to working on his innovations than he might have wished. But he knew that this particular *combination* of problems was important to his organizational public. Moreover, this set of problems posed a potential threat to the ability of the schools to carry out their most important routine, classroom teaching.

Foster, however, continued to enjoy strong community support. Indeed, despite the emergence of a new and serious problem, and within a few months of his strongly worded letter to the *Oakland Tribune,* the Board of Education offered, and Foster accepted, a new four-year contract which included a raise in salary. Neither of these actions provoked a public outcry. Nor did the limited success of Foster's attempts at innovation diminish his attractiveness to others in the educational profession. That is to say, Foster's decision to stay in Oakland was not prompted by a lack of alternatives. Another superintendent's post and a senior appointment at a nearby university had been offered shortly before he accepted Oakland's new contract.

Disappointment over the limited progress toward his goals might have led to some thoughts of resignation. But Foster refused to admit defeat. And in his judgment, resigning, even to take another position, would be just that. Perhaps there was an additional consideration. By staying in Oakland Dr. Foster might have believed it would be possible to prove the anonymous "they" referred to in his letter to the *Tribune* to be wrong about the capabilities of black administrators. And finally there were elements of personal and professional pride involved. Foster was deeply committed to urban education; it was both his career and his profession. Leaving an unfinished task for a successor was, in his view, unprofessional conduct. In personal terms, Foster's self-esteem might have received a blow if a replacement were to achieve success where Foster had not. In any event, Foster did not leave Oakland and he did not abandon his commitment to change in the Oakland public schools. Together with his key staff, the superintendent continued to assure the Board of Education and the public that they were hard at work making the system "fly."

During his three years in Oakland, Superintendent Foster sought to combine two, perhaps contradictory, conceptions of the political executive's responsibilities. On the one hand he viewed himself as his organization's "change-agent." His actions with regard to the start of innovations appear to be consistent with Selznick's ideas about redefining organizational purpose and character.[3] In addition, Foster, as Herbert Simon has noted, had to be the innovator, who has a special duty to attend to "creative" problem solving for the organization.[4] By filling this role, the executive becomes a stimulus for others within the organization to release their own creative energies. Such formulations of the leadership role seem to imply that "whatever the source of the leader's ideas, he cannot inspire his people unless he expresses . . . goals and aims which in some sense they want."[5] While these ideas do not fully embrace the core of the "human relations" approach to management, they do imply a more co-operative style of leadership than is normally associated with the classic hierarchical distribution of authority in formal organizations.

No one seriously questioned the political executive's responsibility to introduce innovations, or to make the critical decisions their adoption would require. Because of his own belief that the executive as "change-agent" should not be involved in "operations," however, Foster delegated substantial responsibilities for implementation to the associate superintendents. In other words,

3. Philip Selznick, *Leadership in Administration*, (New York: Harper & Row, 1957), chapter 2.

4. Herbert A. Simon, "The Decision Maker as Innovator" in *Concepts and Issues in Administrative Behavior*, ed. Sidney Mallick and Edward Van Ness (Englewood Clifs, N.J.: Prentice-Hall, 1962), pp. 66-69.

5. David C. McClelland, "The Two Faces of Power," *Journal of International Affairs* 24, no. 1 (1970): 38.

he treated innovations not as critical decisions but as a series of routine duty assignments to his key subordinates. In some cases, perhaps, the issue of delegation might not deserve much attention, but when an organization is being moved toward new ways of task performance and definition, delegation itself becomes a critical decision. If the innovations had been treated as discrete entities, the assignments of specific responsibilities to the individual associate superintendents would not have put implementation at risk. But community involvement, decentralization and the program budget were not independent in Foster's thinking. He consistently stressed his belief that these changes constituted a single, comprehensive policy for the management of big-city school systems. The three programs were presented as a unit for board consideration. The board gave its approval because Foster was persuasive, not because the interdependencies among the components were fully explained.

Another weakness revealed by the Oakland experience is the difficulty imposed upon efforts to change by organizational poverty. The constraints on innovation within the schools were most severe in the areas of decentralization and PPBS. It is worth recalling in this connection that Foster's success with community involvement was significantly aided by the external foundation support which he was able to secure for the Master Plan Citizens Committee. No such assistance was available for either of the additional programs. Thus it would seem that resource deficiencies often exacerbate the normal difficulties which are expected to accompany attempts at organizational change. For public bureaucracies, dependent upon tax levies for their revenues, there does not appear to be any immediate solution to the dilemma. Foster believed that organizational change was possible within the resource constraints which existed when he took over as the head of the school system. In addition, he expected that those changes would help to convert public dissatisfaction, as shown by the history of failure on tax and bond issues, into support for his claims for additional revenues. We have seen, however, that the campaign for a tax increase under his administration also met with defeat. Foster, too, learned that there were limits to environmental permissiveness.

Few political executives consider themselves to be "theorists" of organizations. Too often they view this expression as implying *leisurely* reflection and study. Like Foster, these individuals believe they have no time for such activities. What is usually meant by those who want organizational leaders to be theorists is little more than what William F. Whyte had in mind in suggesting that the executive

can act more effectively if he recognizes the organization models he carries around in his head and tests them against the realities of experience.[6]

The management policy which Foster sought to introduce was broad in scope, embracing not merely the organization, but a substantial part of the external political environment as well. The innovations implied a totally new relationship between organizations and their public. And it was this unique conception, of transforming a public organization into an integral part of the citizens' lives, which Foster had been unable to make clear. Yet this was the central idea in his references to the schools as "community institutions." Community involvement and decentralization were means to that end. These changes would provide a way for the development of systematic exchanges between the organization and the environment which would be a tacit statement of their interdependence. More important, from Foster's point of view, was his expectation that once recognized, interdependence would turn into an exchange of resources leading to the improved academic performance of students which he had promised.

As George Gallup reminded us earlier, the public tends not to judge its political executives too harshly when their performances don't quite match their promises. Still, it was the ambition and vision of his proposals for change which had made Dr. Foster an attractive candidate for the vacant post. It did not matter that the full scope of Foster's vision for the future of urban education was not fully understood by Oakland's citizens. What the public understood very well was Marcus Foster's dedication to his profession and his commitment to changing public education for the better. Oakland had a superintendent who was energetic and capable of stimulating support for a public bureaucracy on the basis of his own persuasive idealism. Foster was able to

6. William F. Whyte, "Models for Building and Changing Organizations," *Human Organization* 26, nos. 1 & 2 (Summer 1967): 22.

inspire his staff and his public to believe that grand objectives could be realized. He was able to convince these audiences that reach must always exceed the ability to grasp. This is a difficult legacy to assess, for it is not entirely tangible. But it is that special quality by which we differentiate successful leaders and which reconciles us to an awareness of our own limitations.

Epilogue

On 6 November 1973, marcus A. Foster, the superintendent of schools in Oakland, California, was assassinated. His deputy, Robert Blackburn, was critically wounded, but he recovered.

School board members reacted strongly:

"It's like when Kennedy was assassinated . . ."
"This is the greatest loss the City of Oakland has ever known . . ."
"[He gave] so much leadership, so much warmth, so much charisma . . . he was just like a Pied Piper. People just came to him."
(Quoted in the Oakland Tribune, 7 November 1973)

An urban guerilla group calling itself the "Symbionese Liberation Army" claimed credit for the shooting, which occurred as Foster and Blackburn were leaving the weekly meeting of Oakland's Board of Education. The SLA sent a letter to a local radio station stating that they had "executed" Foster because he had supported a controversial student identification program.

This political assassination of an educator whose mission was not political tragically ended Marcus A. Foster's life, and with it his experiment in open leadership and organizational innovation.

Index

"Administrator": Board of Education sees superintendent as, rather than as policy-maker, 20-21; as leadership style, 2n-3n

Adrian, Charles, 14n

"Agitator," as leadership style, 2-3

Alameda County Taxpayers Association, 35

Almond, Gabriel A., 32n

Altshuler, Alan A., 52n

American Association of School Administrators, 149

Anthony, Robert N., 130n

Asian-American community, and Foster, 57-59

Assistant superintendent for elementary instruction, 73-74, 83, 84

Assistant superintendent for secondary instruction, 74, 83

Assistant superintendent for urban educational services, 74, 84

Assistant superintendents: as inherited "leadership core," 73-75; under new cabinet organization, 83-87

Associate superintendent for educational development and services, 83, 84, 86-87, 110-111. See also Cabinet

Associate superintendent for management systems, 83, 84-85; criteria for selection of, 86-87; and conflict with comptroller, 141-42; on PPBS goals and implementation, 136-39. See also Cabinet

Associate superintendent for planning, research and evaluation, 83, 84; in budget process, 91-92; criteria for selection of, 86-87; organizational link to Foster, 87, 91-92; on PPBS, 136; staff needs of, 149. See also Cabinet

Associate superintendents (regional), 9, 84; as Foster's "alter egos," 88, 92-93, 100, 105; conflict between Foster and Board of Education over selection of, 107, 108-109; and community relations, 117, 118; criteria for selection of, 86-87 and day-to-day administration, 87-88, 92, 118; effort of, to control special education programs, 110-12, 146; lack of adequate power or resources in decentralized system, 109-13, 115, 118, 146-47; lack of sufficient staff, 116, 149; and principals, 88, 93, 131; role under decentralized system, 99-100, 105-107, 151-52; role in reorganized cabinet, 88-89, 93, 114 table; view of PPBS, 135-36. See also Cabinet

Bailey, F. G., 45

Baker, Helen, 98n

Banfield, Edward C., 4n, 26n

Barnard, Chester, 92

Barnes, Louis B., 117n-118n

Baum, Bernard H., 98n, 113

Benbow, Dr. Spencer, 73, 84-85, 107, 122-23

Biller, Robert P., 6n

Billingsley, Andrew, 24

Black Caucus, 31, 35, 37; claims of, to represent unified black community, 36; and control of OEO and Model Cities funds, 18-19; relations with Foster, 1-2, 49-50, 59, 60; role in selection of new superintendent, 13-14, 24, 25, 33-34, 35-36, 43; and second screening committee, 34n-35n; teacher support for, 26, 33

Blacks: activism among, 1-2, 12-13, 59; in Foster's cabinet, 74-75, 81, 84, 93; Foster's constituency-building among middle class, 59; in Oakland student body, 17; and pluralism in school bureaucracy, 3-4; reaction to Blackburn, 76-77; response to Foster's decentralization plan, 108-109

Blackburn, Robert, 56, 155; on decentralization plans, 102; and PPBS, 121, 135; and regional associate superintendents, 87, 88; relation with Foster, 80-81, 87, 90; as risk-taker, 76, 80-81; role in reorganized cabinet, 78-80

Board of Education: and budget process, 32-33, 140-42; choice of James J. Mason as superintendent, 22-27; choice of Foster as superintendent, 38-43; concerned about school tax election during selection process, 22, 22n-23n; functional constituencies of members of, 30-31, 31n; limitations of access to diverse views about schools, 32-33; narrow, apolitical construal of school problems and groups, 17-18, 20, 26-27, 32; and PPBS, 120, 138-40; reaction to decentralization plan, 99, 103-104, 107-109; relations with Foster, 56-57, 70, 77, 91, 108-109; response to new selection process for principals, 53; self-image as representing public interest, 14, 27, 30-32; social composition of, 27, 30; and screening committees, 13, 18-19, 34-35; view of cabinet decision making as not accountable, 75-76; view of community involvement as means to lessen dissent, 70; view of proper role for community in selection process, 13-15, 27, 34; view of selection process as non-political, 26-27; view of superintendent's qualifications and tasks, 8, 16-17, 19-21, 27

Bonds, school, 28-29 table, 126. *See also* Taxes, school

Braibanti, Ralph, 4

Bret Harte Junior High School, 106

Brown Act, 23n

Brzezinski, Zbigniew, 30n

Buchanan, Keith, 64n

Budget director, 83-84; and PPBS, 125

Budget process: Board of Education view of, as policymaking, 32-33; business manager's role in, 140, 141-42; as complicating factor during search for new superintendent, 18, 32-33; fiscal dependence as constraint on, 126-27; Foster's involvement in, 91-92, 140, 142; impact of PPBS on, 136-42, 147-48; in Price-Waterhouse recommendations, 83-84; reform of, complicated by state requirements, 139-40, 141-42. *See also* PPBS

Bukhead, Jesse, 6

Burns, James MacGregor, 60, 61, 73n

Business community: and economy and efficiency in school administration, 5-6, 120; Foster's contacts with, 56-57

Business manager, 73, 83, 140, 141-42. *See also* Benbow, Dr. Spencer

Businessmen, taboo on involvement of, in political contests, 30n

Cabinet: not accountable, in view of Board of Education, 75-76; decision making in, 88-94; Foster's strategy to reorganize, 72-75, 82-83, 95-96; and planning for decentralization, 100-104; and planning for PPBS, 132, 147-48; reorganization of, 83-88; use of, by Foster to implement rather than formulate policy, 88-91, 93-94. *See also* various Associate superintendents

Caiden, Naomi, 129n

California Association of School Administrators, 34

California Department of Education, and PPBS, 124-25

California School Boards' Association, 34

California State Legislature: and decentralization, 103-104; and evaluation of teacher performance, 134; and school tax policy, 126-27; and support of PPBS, 123, 125, 127

Capozzola, John M., 134

Carey, Dr. William, 134-35

Carlson, Jack W., 133

Carlson, Richard O., 38n, 42, 71, 72n, 73n

Carmichael, Stokely, 52n

Castlemont and Oakland Technical Area (Region 1), 102, 103, 104

Castlemont and Skyline Areas (Region 3), 102, 103, 104

Chase Manhattan Bank, on expense of PPBS, 131

Choucri, Nazli, 95

City Council of Oakland, 66-68

Clark, Burton R., 27n

Cleveland, Harlan, 69

Community control, 52n; Foster contrasts, with community involvement, 52-53, 61. *See also* Community involvement

Community involvement: as answer to insularity of public bureaucracies, 144; Board of Education view of, as means to lessen dissent, 70; as "cost-free," 95-96, 145, 152; decentralization as extension of, 96, 117-18; Master Plan Citizens Committee as vehicle of, 9, 61-64; as non-radical, 145-46; versus community control, 52-53, 61; as recognition of ecological connection between school and community, 4-5, 146; role of, in Foster's plans to change organization of education, 3, 6, 10, 46-47,